THE COMPLETE TOOLKIT FOR FIRST TIME DADS

FROM PREGNANCY TO NEWBORN CARE
NAVIGATE CHILDBIRTH, EMBRACE EMOTIONAL
WELL-BEING, AND BALANCE WORK AND
FAMILY TO PREPARE FOR FATHERHOOD

SAMUEL EMERSON

TABLE OF CONTENTS

PART III
NEWBORN AND INFANT CARE

INTRODUCTION

So you've just found out that you're about to be a Dad? Congratulations! This can be such an exciting time in your life! It can also, however, be very confusing and nerve-wracking. They say a woman becomes a mother the day she finds out that she's pregnant, but a man only becomes a father when he holds his child for the first time. This is probably because so much of the pregnancy revolves around your partner. The idea of becoming a parent may feel surreal to you at the moment. You can't see the baby, and unlike your partner, their impending arrival hasn't started to affect your life yet. But that doesn't mean you can't prepare.

I know how left out you probably feel right now. Everyone is so focused on their partner and their growing belly that almost nobody gives attention to Dad. Well, this is your time to shine! If you've been looking for ways to become more involved in the pregnancy process and have been wondering how best to support your partner through this transition, look no further! In this book, we'll be demystifying pregnancy for you, going week by week. I'll let you in on the secrets to keeping your partner as comfortable as possible as her body goes through the transformative process of creating life. We'll give you a peek into what's going on in her belly because you're probably not getting much from those confusing black-and-white images that she keeps telling you are pictures of your growing baby! From morning sickness to heartburn, I'll also be sharing some trade secrets and recipes to help your partner cope with some of those uncomfortable side effects of pregnancy. And prepare for the hormones because they'll be affecting you, too!

Are you terrified at the idea of having to care for a newborn? That's okay; I'll be guiding you through those early days, too. From nappy changes to feeding times, there are so many hands-on ways you can be a helpful co-parent while your partner recovers from giving birth. Speaking of giving birth, what's the deal with that? Trust me, Hollywood does nothing to prepare you for that incredible experience! Take a prenatal class with me as we delve into the complex process of birthing. From guiding your partner through her contractions to holding her hand through that final push, let's enter the delivery room together and find out what you can expect on the big day!

Becoming a Dad is something that's going to change your life; there's no doubt about that. It's normal to be anxious about the future and worried about uncertainties. Let's try to soothe some of that fear by equipping you with the information you'll need to embark on this journey with confidence. These months are going to set the tone for your parenting journey, so give yourself the best start possible. There's no such thing as a perfect parent, so don't be too hard on yourself if you mess up sometimes. That's how we learn. Don't forget that as important as it is for you to support your partner along this journey, you'll need some support, too. After all, they say it takes a village to raise a child. Make sure your village is made up of people you can turn to in times of crisis and with whom you can share all those exciting milestones. What are milestones? We'll get to that too. When it comes to small things like your baby taking their first steps or sitting up for the first time, you're going to experience a range of emotions you've never felt before! I never thought seeing a baby roll over could fill me with so much joy and wonder before I became a father.

In addition to strengthening your relationship with your partner, becoming a parent is going to change you in more ways than you can imagine. There are going to be highs and lows, and how you navigate them will determine the future of your parenting journey. Learn to roll with the punches and always trust your gut. Try not to take the things people say too personally. When it comes to parenting, everyone and their uncle are going to have something to say. Unwarranted advice just comes with the territory. Complete strangers will try to tell you that you're not holding the baby correctly or show you the best way to calm down your crying child. Take it on the chin, and don't let it get to you. At the end of the day, you know yourself, and you know what's best for your child. Remember that.

Most of all, appreciate the little things. It might not seem like it now, but these are moments you'll cherish forever. They're only small for such a short time, so make the most of all the moments you get to spend with your little one. Get all the love and cuddles you can before they're old enough to tell you that you're embarrassing them! Treasure these early days. You have to build a lifelong bond with your child and never pass up an opportunity to strengthen that connection. And never take it for granted that you've been blessed with the sacred task of being a father. It's a long journey, and it's not always going to be easy. But I can promise you that every second will be worth it.

PART I

THE PREGNANCY JOURNEY

1

UNDERSTANDING PREGNANCY—A WEEK-BY-WEEK COMPANION

As dad-to-be, your primary job is to make sure mom-to-be doesn't see red during this stressful time of emotional and physical upheaval for her and to do your part to make the pregnancy as successful as possible.

— JOHN PFEIFFER

THOSE NINE MONTHS of pregnancy can feel like a lifetime. There's both too much time to wait and not enough time to prepare! One moment, you're discussing colors for a nursery, and then it's like you blink, and suddenly, she's gone into labor. I'm here to fill in those gaps for you and help you navigate the rough terrain of pregnancy. Make no mistake, it's going to take as much of a toll on you as it will on your partner, even though you're not the one carrying the baby.

In this chapter, we'll be breaking down the pregnancy into its three trimesters, following along with the growth of the baby and how these changes and developments will affect your partner. Having a better grasp on what's going on will better equip you to be able to support her during this time. There are obvious physical changes, like her belly preventing her from being able to bend over and pick up her water bottle when she's dropped it; those are easy enough to figure out. But when she starts crying because she doesn't want you to help her pick up the water bottle, well, those changes might not be as easy to handle. But don't worry, I've got your back!

The First Trimester

The first 3 months of pregnancy are referred to as the first trimester. Although your partner won't physically look pregnant yet, she'll probably go through some of the more severe symptoms during this time. You must do your best to help her adjust to her pregnancy and ease into the new pace that her life is going to take. Do as much for her as she'll allow you to while still allowing her to do what she feels she needs to. It's not easy for a mom to accept that she can't do things on her own anymore, so don't feel offended if your help goes unappreciated or is met with disdain. This adjustment is as difficult for her as it is for you, but I'm sure you'll find your feet together eventually. In the meantime, let's look at what you can expect.

Week 1 and 2

This early in the pregnancy, there's no baby yet, and your partner probably doesn't even know they're pregnant. Although conception has taken place, the physical signs of pregnancy are either minimal or non-existent. You and your partner are, as yet, blissfully unaware of the miracle unfolding in her uterus.

Week 3 and 4

The fertilized egg moves to the uterus, and implantation occurs. That's just a fancy way of saying your baby has found its new home for the next 8 months and is starting to form. Right now, your baby is the size of a sesame seed.

Around this time, your partner might begin to notice mild symptoms of early pregnancy, such as a little fatigue and breast tenderness. She may also have missed her period. This is a good time to consider taking a pregnancy test, as most tests can pick up on pregnancy after 4 weeks.

You can support your partner through this potentially confusing time by reassuring them that everything will be fine and that their feelings are valid. You might be getting a little jittery yourself, and that's normal!

Week 5

This week, your baby is the size of an orange seed. (Around 0.13 inches or 0.3 cm)

They've started growing little arms and legs, and their hearts have started beating! It's a great time to schedule your first doctor's appointment.

Your partner will likely be experiencing pregnancy symptoms in full force now. Extreme fatigue to the point where they can barely keep their eyes open, nausea, and needing the bathroom every two minutes are going to become the order of the day. The term *morning sickness* can be very misleading because bouts of severe nausea actually happen at any time of the day. Sometimes all day.

You can help your partner combat the nausea by making sure she eats frequently, because an empty stomach can make the nausea much worse. Smoothies are a good way to keep her nourished if she's struggling to eat through full meals. Keep some healthy snacks nearby to offer her whenever she gets peckish. Tag along to her doctor's appointment for emotional support and to get to witness the miracle of life! Hearing that heartbeat for the first time isn't something you'll want to miss or ever forget.

Week 6

Your baby has grown to the size of a paperclip (about 0.2 inches or 0.5 cm) and is starting to develop their facial features, brain, and muscles.

Your partner's pregnancy symptoms have probably kicked into overdrive by now, and, as a result, she can't really do much of anything. Aside from the exhaustion, her hormones probably have her moods moving at hyperspeed, and you might feel like you're getting whiplash from it. She can go from anger to laughter in a matter of seconds, so be warned and be prepared.

You might feel like you're walking on eggshells, but I promise, it will pass. This is just as hard on her as it is on you, so don't take it to heart when she snaps at you for minor errors. Those baby hormones are really doing a number on her. You can make her life easier by taking on more chores around the house, especially cleaning out the cat litter if you have a cat. Cat poop contains toxins in it that can be potentially harmful to both her and your unborn baby. It's better to be safe than sorry!

Week 7

Your baby is now the size of a wireless earbud (around 0.3 inches or 0.7 cm), and their umbilical cord has formed.

Your partner's sense of smell will become your worst enemy this week, so keep any strong odors to a minimum. Maybe bypass wearing your favorite cologne for a while until the smell doesn't send her running for the bathroom. She might also be struggling with heartburn, bloating, and an unnecessarily excessive amount of saliva. Keep these things in mind when preparing meals.

Aside from removing any offending smells from anywhere within a ten-mile radius, you can support your partner by just listening. She's probably going to have a lot to whine and complain about, so let her. Let her vent, cry, and feel sorry for herself, and don't forget to remind her that she's still beautiful and that you still love her. Also, a glass of milk does wonders for heartburn.

Week 8

Your baby is now the size of a Lego brick (around 0.6 inches or 1.5 cm) and is growing their own little fingers and toes.

Your baby isn't the only one growing this week; your partner might begin picking up some weight, but don't point it out! Around this time, she might start developing aversions to certain kinds of food, so make sure to keep the offending items out of sight. You should also ensure that she's replacing the nutrients from those foods with other things that are less offensive to her sensitive palate.

Your partner is probably starting to feel more connected to the pregnancy at this point, so be sure to match her excitement. Smile at the scans she keeps showing you, even if you're not sure what you're looking at, and spend hours discussing potential baby names. Despite the hormones wreaking havoc on her, this is still an exciting time for your relationship, so enjoy it!

Week 9

This week, your baby is the size of a cherry. (Around 0.9 inches, or 2.2 cm). All of their essential body parts have formed, and they're beginning to move, although your partner won't be able to feel that for quite some time yet.

Your partner's belly hasn't started to grow yet, but their breasts have probably become a lot fuller. Be careful when showing your appreciation, however, because this growth comes with extreme tenderness, and the slightest touch might earn you an angry hiss. Morning sickness will probably peak around this time, along with that incapacitating fatigue, so be gentle with them.

Offering your partner some dry crackers before they get out of bed in the morning can really help with the nausea. Ginger has also been proven to be a great natural remedy for morning sickness. Keep them hydrated and encourage them to eat a little every few hours instead of trying to stick to regular meals.

Week 10

Your baby is now the size of a bottle cap (around 1.2 inches or 3 cm), and all their vital organs are fully functional. This week, they'll start swallowing and kicking, too. However, again, it's still some time before your partner detects these movements.

The worst is over! This week, the more severe pregnancy symptoms will begin to subside, but that doesn't mean it's time to break out the bubbly! Remember, your partner should abstain completely from alcohol throughout her pregnancy, and you might want to show some solidarity by following suit. If you're a smoker, now would probably be a good time to quit as well because secondhand smoke isn't good for your partner or unborn child either.

Around this time, your partner will probably start going to regular doctor's appointments; do your best to tag along. Aside from getting to share these amazing experiences with her, it will also give you an opportunity to get advice from her doctor on what her needs may be and how you can best help her meet them.

Week 11

Your fully formed baby is now the size of a USB flash drive (around 1.6 inches or 4 cm). Their fingers and toes have separated and their nail beds and hair follicles have started developing.

Your partner might get a new lease on life with her energy levels restored. Encourage her to use this energy sparingly and not to overdo it. She'll probably still be running back and forth to the bathroom pretty frequently, though.

You can make your partner's many nightly trips to the bathroom a little less risky by adding a few nightlights along the way and moving anything that might trip her on her path.

Week 12

Your baby is now roughly the size of an AA battery (around 2 inches or 5 cm), and their reflexes are coming along too. They can open and close their fingers and also make sucking motions.

Your partner can expect the beginning of a baby bump to start showing this week, which is an incredibly exciting developmental milestone! Her rapidly changing body might lead to a decreased sex drive and some slight insecurities, so be sensitive to that.

You can be a supportive partner during this time by sharing in the wonder of your partner's developing pregnancy and reassuring her that the changes to her body don't negatively influence your perceptions of her. Be involved when it comes to doctor appointments and scans, and make time to help your partner address any concerns she might have surrounding the pregnancy. The risk of miscarriage falls significantly at 12 weeks, which is a huge relief!

The Second Trimester

The second trimester is kind of the sweet spot when it comes to pregnancy. Most of the severe physical symptoms that made those early weeks unbearable for your partner have significantly subsided, and her belly hasn't gotten big enough for it to make her life too uncomfortable yet. She'll probably also feel a lot more energetic during this time. Use that energy to your advantage by making as many preparations for the baby's arrival as you can. It might still feel like a long way away, but trust me, the time will go by so fast!

Week 13

Your baby is the size of a matchbox (around 2.9 inches or 7.3 cm) and even has their own fingerprints now!

Your partner might be starting to look less bloated and more pregnant now, which is exciting. Her energies are restored, and she's probably talking about the baby nonstop. Let her!

At this point, you might need to show more enthusiasm about the baby because your partner might be nervous that she's annoying you with all the baby talk. So be the first one to introduce the subject! It's also probably a good time to start helping her shop for some maternity wear.

Week 14

Your golf ball-sized baby (around 3.4 inches or 8.6 cm) is becoming a lot cuter this week and might even start sucking their thumb.

Your partner is settling into the pregnancy and feeling a lot more comfortable now. Perhaps it's a good time to start introducing some moderate exercise, like going for walks—nothing too strenuous.

You might need some support yourself now! Couvade syndrome, also known as sympathetic pregnancy, affects about half of fathers. It basically means you're not going crazy if you find yourself experiencing the same pregnancy symptoms as your partner. You might find yourself fighting for the spot beside her in the toilet bowl the next time you get a sniff of a raw egg!

Week 15

Sitting about the size of a computer mouse (around 4 inches or 10.1 cm), your baby's movements have become a lot more fluid now, and their bones are getting stronger.

Your partner may experience an increase in her appetite this week, so make sure you're prepared with a fridge stocked with healthy snacks. She may also experience the first fluttering in her belly, another exciting milestone in her pregnancy!

Week 16

This week, your baby's about the size of a smartphone (around 4.5 inches or 11.4 cm), and their eyes can move around.

Your partner might experience some dizzy spells as a result of the increased volume of blood in her body, so remind her to watch her step. Her growing baby bump will probably be getting her more excited and eliciting a lot of comments and smiles, giving her more confidence.

Be sure to keep an eye on her, ready to offer a steady hand in the case of dizzy spells because they come out of nowhere. It's also a good time to start throwing out some ideas for baby names.

Week 17

Now, at the size of a video game controller (around 5 inches or 12.7 cm), your baby is probably a lot more active in there, and their hearing has developed as well.

Your partner's hormones are running wild again this week, and she might begin to experience swelling in her hands and feet. Constantly having a blocked nose might lead to her snoring at night as well, but don't worry, this is only temporary.

You can support your partner by encouraging her to elevate her feet when she's sitting down. Maybe break out the massage oil and offer her a foot rub too. For the snoring, getting a humidifier to run in your bedroom at night while you sleep will help ease her blocked nose.

Week 18

The size of your baby this week is about the same as a TV remote (around 5.6 inches or 14.2 cm). Their nervous system is also becoming a lot more developed, giving them the ability to yawn, hiccup, and swallow.

Your partner is probably feeling the baby's movements a lot more distinctly now, especially when they kick! She'll likely be experiencing a lot of aches and pains as a result of her growing uterus as well.

You can support your partner by continuing to offer massages for those aching muscles. It's also a good time to start bonding with the baby by talking to her belly and singing to it as well; the baby can now hear you!

Week 19

Your baby is the size of a dollar bill this week (around 6 inches or 15.2 cm), and their senses are developing.

Your partner will probably be restless at night due to increased activity from the baby. She'll also have some pain and discomfort from the growth of her uterus.

You can support your partner by helping her find comfortable positions to sleep in or by getting her a pregnancy pillow. You might be relegated to the couch for the sake of her being able to get a good night's sleep.

Week 20

Your baby is about the size of a banana (around 6.5 inches or 16.5 cm) and is getting a lot more active this week.

Now that you're officially halfway through the pregnancy, your partner will go for her 20-week ultrasound. This scan is to assess the baby's anatomy and make sure they're growing and developing at a healthy rate. She may even leave with a cute scan to show off!

Tag along to the appointment if you can. It's a good opportunity for you to share the wonder of experiencing the ultrasound and getting to see your baby moving around. You'll also get the lowdown from the doctor about how your partner can best continue to care for herself and her growing baby during the pregnancy. Don't be scared to bring a list of questions with you.

Week 21

This week, your baby is the size of a water bottle. (around 10.5 inches or 26.6 cm). They've also started sleeping and waking up at regular intervals.

Be prepared for those pregnancy cravings because they come in full force. Your partner's growing appetite might be a reason for buying a few extra groceries. Remember, it's not about eating more food but taking in more calories to sustain the growing baby. Your partner might also begin to experience Braxton Hicks, which are simulated contractions.

You can support your partner by reading up about Braxton Hicks's contractions and being there to reassure her that the baby is fine whenever they happen. You'll also likely be sent to the store several times when she decides that she must have a certain food item immediately, lest she perish! In these situations, it's best not to argue and just go along with it.

Week 22

Your baby is the size of a small football this week (around 11 inches or 27.9 cm) and has fully developed eyes.

Your partner will be experiencing more pronounced movements in her uterus, which might cause discomfort. Her growing belly is probably starting to get in the way of things, and the strain of pregnancy is starting to affect her general mobility and energy levels.

You can support your partner by taking over tasks that have become too difficult for them to do on their own. Encourage them to rest as much as possible and make sure they stay properly nourished and hydrated.

Week 23

Your book-sized bundle of joy (around 11.4 inches or 28.9 cm) is now able to recognize sounds. If you talk to them, they might move!

Your partner is probably starting to feel a little top-heavy at this point. Her belly is starting to take a toll on her back, and she might be experiencing some issues with her skin, such as pigmentation.

You can support your partner by giving her some back rubs. It also might be a good idea to buy a pregnancy support belt that will relieve some of the strain on her back for the rest of the pregnancy. They're generally very cheap and available from your local drugstore.

Week 24

Measuring around the length of a ruler, baby's (around 12 inches or 30.4 cm) brain is developing rapidly this week. Their little lungs are also developing, though they have yet to fully mature.

Your partner's lungs, however, are taking a bit of a beating now that her uterus is taking up so much space. She might find herself frequently suffering from shortness of breath as a result of this. Baby's movements are now visible from the outside as well, so you can finally get in on the action!

You can support your partner by helping her find comfortable positions that will make breathing easier and aid her in feeling less suffocated. While she's lying down, take the opportunity to try and see if you can spot the baby moving! Sharing this experience will not only strengthen your bond with your partner as parents but also give you a chance to feel more involved in the pregnancy. The more you talk with your baby, the higher the chances they'll recognize your voice when they're born.

Week 25

Your baby is now about the same size as a rutabaga (around 13.6 inches or 34.5 cm), and their skin is starting to look more like skin. They're also starting to grow hair.

Your partner is probably really starting to feel the strain from the pregnancy now that her belly's getting much bigger. An increase in her blood supply might cause visible veins, and she'll also experience swelling in her hands and feet.

Encourage her to rest with her feet elevated to help ease some of the swelling and make sure she stays properly hydrated. Don't forget those foot rubs!

Week 26

About the size of a laptop keyboard (around 14 inches or 35.5 cm), your baby's eyes have now opened, and they're able to react to sounds and lights.

Your partner will likely be suffering from sleepless nights. This is both a result of her discomfort and also of the baby moving around. Babies are more active when their mothers aren't moving, which unfortunately means the baby moves around the most when your partner is trying to get some sleep.

You can support your partner by helping her create a comfortable sleep environment. Make sure she has enough pillows supporting her back and belly to make sleeping less strenuous.

Week 27

Your baby is the same size as a head of cauliflower (around 14.4 inches or 36.5 cm), and they're becoming more active, doing lots of stretching and kicking.

Your partner's growing size may be imposing limits on her mobility and affecting her balance and coordination. Heartburn and indigestion might also be causing her a lot of discomfort. The stretching skin on her belly will be very itchy, but tell her not to scratch it, as this will only make it worse.

You can support your partner by rubbing some shea butter over her belly to soothe the itching and moisturize the drying skin. Be sure to offer a helping hand if she needs to bend over or if she's struggling to reach something. Make sure she avoids eating foods that are high in fat or anything too spicy; this will ease the heartburn and indigestion.

The Third Trimester

The end is in sight! This last stretch can feel like an eternity as you eagerly await the arrival of your baby. Last-minute purchases of nursery essentials and signing up for prenatal classes can make the upcoming changes feel a lot more real to you now than they did a few months ago. When it comes to your partner, this is probably the most physically draining stage of pregnancy, as her growing belly makes daily life a constant battle. Try to do as much for her as you can, but don't forget to take time for yourself as well. When the baby arrives, they'll be taking up all your time and attention for a while.

Week 28

Your baby is now the same size as a loaf of bread (around 14.8 inches or 37.5 cm). They've grown their own eyelashes and can blink.

Your partner is probably getting tired more easily and is frequently out of breath. The strain on her body is making her more lethargic, so encourage her to rest and take it easy.

If you haven't yet, sign yourself and your partner up for some prenatal classes. Preparing for the birth will make it less daunting, and you'll also be able to connect with other couples who are expecting and get some advice. It will also be really helpful for you to be able to talk to other dads about your experiences.

Week 29

Now, the size of a butternut squash (around 15.2 inches or 38.6 cm), your baby is starting to feel a little cramped. Their muscles and lungs continue to mature and develop.

Your partner is probably so over being pregnant at this point. She hardly has the energy to do anything, and finding a comfortable sleeping position has become nearly impossible.

Be as supportive as possible during these last few weeks. Take over as much of the household chores and responsibilities as you can, and consider taking some time off work to help with the final preparations for the baby's arrival. There won't be much time to buy or get things once the baby is here.

Week 30

Your baby is now the size of a large cabbage (around 15.7 inches or 39.8 cm) and their brain is developing rapidly. It can turn its head and make facial expressions, too!

Your partner is likely having more frequent Braxton-Hicks contractions now as her body prepares for labor. Be sure to remain calm when this happens and try to keep her as relaxed as possible. She's going to think she's going into labor every time this happens, so be patient and understanding. Aches and pains will become the order of the day as the baby grows as well, especially in her back and legs.

You can support your partner by helping her do some leg stretches and basic exercises when her muscles start to cramp. Remember, you can never give too many back massages or foot rubs. They will always be appreciated!

Week 31

This week, your baby is the size of a bowling ball (around 16.2 inches or 41.1 cm). Their senses are fully developed, and they're starting to put on some weight.

Your partner is going to be extremely uncomfortable for these last few weeks. With the baby forcing her organs into a cramped space, she's probably going to struggle with things like shortness of breath and needing the bathroom often. She'll also change her posture as a result of her growing belly, making her coordination even worse than before.

You can support your partner by making your home more accessible. You can do this by removing any rugs or carpets that she might slip on or by installing a handle in your bathroom near the toilet so she can help herself get up more easily.

Week 32

Your baby is about the size of a shoe box now (around 16.7 inches or 42.4 cm) and is fully formed. They're also starting to practice breathing.

Your partner might start nesting. Never heard of it? It's a bit of a frenzy where she feels the urge to prepare for the baby's arrival. You might find her obsessing about the nursery, cleaning endlessly, and stressing about baby-proofing the house. Despite this, her size is still making mobility a nightmare.

You can support your partner by helping her get things done. Take over the more demanding tasks, but don't deprive her of the need to partake. Encourage her enthusiasm and get on board!

Week 33

Baby is the size of a pineapple this week (around 17.2 inches or 43.6 cm), a very uncomfortable one at that!

Your partner's thoughts have probably turned towards the birth, so start planning around that. Make sure you're aware of her birth plan and that all of the necessary people have a copy as well. Sleep is probably becoming increasingly uncomfortable, so bear with her in these final weeks.

You can support your partner by helping her get ready for the birth. Make sure the baby bag is packed with all the essential items, and don't forget to pack some snacks and a change of clothes for yourself if you plan on staying over.

Week 34

This week, your baby is the size of a cantaloupe (around 17.7 inches or 44.9 cm) and has begun to descend into the birthing position.

As her due date approaches, your partner will probably experience more intense Braxton Hicks, which will no doubt be a cause of both discomfort and anxiety. Attending birthing classes is a great idea around this time so you both feel prepared for what's about to happen.

Find ways to encourage and support your partner through these final weeks. Help soothe her anxieties and match her excitement. Take in as much information as you can during the birthing classes, and don't be afraid to ask questions. Most importantly, make sure you know how your partner would like you to support her on the day.

Week 35

Your baby is the size of a honeydew melon (around 18.2 inches or 46.2 cm) and has fully functioning kidneys.

This week, your partner will struggle with swelling in her feet and ankles. Encourage her to stay off her feet as much as possible. Do anything around the house that needs doing so she doesn't feel the need to do any chores.

As you prepare for the big day, make sure you're familiar with the multiple routes you can take to the hospital or birth center. It wouldn't hurt to do a few trial runs, either. Make sure your gas tank is full. Preparing for the worst but hoping for the best means you should probably carry a gallon of water and some towels with you in your car because you never know what might happen.

Week 36

Your baby's the same size as a head of lettuce (around 18.7 inches or 47.4 cm), and their skin has become nice and smooth.

Your partner is probably experiencing a lot of pressure in her lower abdomen as a result of the baby dropping lower to prepare for birth. This can be pretty painful, so be mindful of that.

Have you put in for leave at work? If not, you should probably get on that! Make sure your boss is aware that you may need to dip out of work at a moment's notice should your partner unexpectedly go into labor.

Week 37

This week, your baby has grown to the size of a two-liter bottle of soda (around 19.1 inches or 48.5 cm). They are fully developed and ready for the big world outside!

Your partner is now officially full-term. This might cause her a bit of anxiety, so be prepared for a few false alarms! Now that the baby has dropped even lower, her bladder might have her running to the bathroom a lot more often.

Be patient with your partner because she's probably very on edge, especially at the slightest hint of labor signs.

Week 38

Your baby is now the size of a leek (around 19.6 inches or 49.7 cm) and continues to pack on layers of fat as the birth approaches.

The waiting is the hardest part for both of you. It's important to be on high alert for any signs of labor, but also keep yourselves busy to distract yourselves in the meantime.

Week 39

There's a small watermelon in her belly this week (around 20 inches or 50.8 cm) as your baby continues to grow.

Emotions are running high as the big day approaches. Take your mind from things by enjoying these last few days you have to spend with each other. Don't do anything too strenuous, but a picnic in the park isn't a bad idea.

Week 40

Baby is now the size of a small pumpkin (around 20.2 inches and 51.3 cm) and fully formed.

Your partner might experience less movement from the baby now that they don't have much space, so don't be alarmed. Only a third of mothers give birth on their due date, so don't worry too much if it comes and goes without her going into labor.

You can use these final days to finish off preparations. Install your car seat if you haven't done that yet, put the final touches on the nursery, and stock the freezer with some premade meals. And then all that's left to do is wait…

You've made it to the end of the pregnancy, but this is only the beginning! Believe it or not, that was the easy part; now the real work begins. Having been a supportive and encouraging partner thus far will definitely have made a world of difference, however. Knowing what's happening to your partner's body will probably make it a lot easier for you to know how to help her along. Understanding what symptoms to look out for at which points and staying on top of those home remedies will make the transformative journey so much easier for both of you.

However, being able to offer comfort and support for the physical aspect of her pregnancy is only part of the process. You also need to be able to emotionally support her. This journey isn't just about the baby; it's also about the impact that having a child is going to have on your relationship. You can use the time during pregnancy to strengthen your bond with your partner and make that transition into parenthood so much more enjoyable. In the next chapter, we'll be exploring ways for you to grow your relationship while she's growing your baby.

2

DEEPENING THE PARTNERSHIP
THROUGH PREGNANCY

Pregnancy is difficult for women but it is even more difficult for men.

— SUSAN CHEEVER

YOU'RE PROBABLY CONFUSED as to why you would try to deepen your emotional connection to your partner during a time in her life when her emotions are so haywire! I can understand your trepidation; trust me, I've been there. At first, I was sure that my partner's pregnancy was going to ruin our relationship. She'd become so different from the person I'd come to know: calm, controlled, and rational. For weeks, I felt like I was walking on eggshells because the smallest thing would set her off. One moment, I was the enemy, and the next, she was hanging off me like a koala. I was so confused!

The thing I had to learn was that this process wasn't about me adjusting to this new emotional version of my partner. It was about me learning how to love her through it, about me putting my own pride and ego aside to figure out how best to help my partner through what was clearly a very intense phase of her life. Relationships aren't strengthened in happy times. It's easy to see forever with someone when things are sunshine and roses. It's the stormy waters where you really earn your stripes, however. It's about knowing how to look through the irrational rage caused by pregnancy hormones and still see the woman you fell in love with.

Knowing that this was temporary helped, I won't lie. But, more than anything, it was realizing that the way I reacted to her and treated her would have just as big of an impact on how she experienced her pregnancy as well. If I was going to look at her like she was unhinged every time she cried over something that I thought was silly, or if I was going to take offense every time she snapped at me over a minor incident, then we were going to feel that way—unhinged and offended. But, if I met these outbursts with love and compassion, if I allowed her to experience those emotions without judgment, and if I demonstrated empathy, she would be less hard on herself. These small changes in my attitude made all the difference! I found that the pregnancy experience became a lot more enjoyable for both of us. It finally felt like we were in this together, and I learned new ways of being a supportive husband that I'd never known before. Our relationship deepened, and our connection grew stronger than it had ever been. By the time the baby arrived, we were more than ready. And it wasn't just about having all the right things in the nursery. We were a team, and we were ready to tackle any challenge that came our way as a united front. We were parents.

In this chapter, we'll be looking at some ways that you can deepen your relationship with your partner throughout the pregnancy experience. And not just that, but how you can be the emotional support that she needs. How you can be her sanity during the moments when she's not quite feeling herself.

Emotional Support During Pregnancy

Being a supportive partner is about more than just holding her hand during birthing class and occasionally telling her to breathe. Supporting your partner through pregnancy starts from the moment you find out she's expecting. It's going to be a highly emotional time for both of you and while you're allowed to express your own feelings, it would help if you could be a sounding board for her as well. Sharing with each other how you're feeling is a good way to foster open communication, and trust me, you'll need that as parents.

If you decide from the outset to be by her side every step of the way, then you need to hold yourself accountable to that, even when things get hard. Be prepared to have awkward and difficult conversations and possibly be forced a little bit out of your comfort zone. Remember, this is new for both of you. You're both scared and confused. Allow this uncertainty to draw you closer together, not create a rift between you.

Be the Calm in the Storm

Emotional support in the first trimester is key because it's those early days when her emotions are really going to do a number on her. You need to be the emotional compass that points her toward the true north when she gets lost in the maze of hormone-fueled emotional outbursts. Her erratic emotions might shock you at first, but remember, they're just as confusing to her and probably a lot more terrifying. Be the one to reassure her that everything is alright and she's not losing her mind. It's perfectly normal to cry when you reach into the packet of crisps and realize that you've eaten them all. You can totally empathize with her devastation.

A great trick I learned early on was to try to make my partner laugh at the absurdity of certain scenarios. Now, I'm not saying all of them, so use your discretion. But sometimes, just taking a step back to show her the humorous side of her outbursts was enough to break the spell and bring her back to reality. Of course, you know your partner better than I do, so you'll know whether this strategy will work for you. But laughter really is the best medicine, and sometimes, the only way to get through some of those tough spots is to find the humor in them.

You know that her hormones are playing with her emotions. She knows that her hormones are playing with her emotions. But, for God's sake, do not point it out! The worst thing you can do when she is experiencing a tantrum is inquire whether or not she is feeling that way due to her baby hormones. Trust me, it's a quick way to get a large, heavy object launched at your head. Never invalidate her feelings by suggesting that they're not rational. Allow her to feel whatever she's feeling, and then allow it to pass. Give her space when she needs it or comfort when she doesn't. Being there for her isn't about trying to fix everything or giving your opinion on everything. Sometimes, she just needs you to be there with her in it, and that's enough.

Show Up And Get Involved

Emotional support also needs to be put into action. Make sure you show up when she needs you, and don't miss out on things that you know are important to her. Go shopping for cribs, even if the idea of spending hours in a baby store makes you cringe. Take time off work to attend baby scans with her. She probably won't say it, but it'll hurt her feelings if you don't.

Your partner wants to feel that you're just as excited about and invested in this pregnancy as she is. The best way to prove to her that you are is to be an active participant in planning and preparing for the baby's arrival. Get your hands dirty painting the nursery. Pretend to know the difference between beige and champagne. Pretend to care what grain of wood the baby changing station is made out of.

And don't just go through the motions; be proactive. Do your own research about things you may need, and then discuss the options with your partner. Despite the fact that it may not mean much to you, why not do it if it will bring her joy? I had no idea how many different shades of yellow existed until my partner became pregnant. I spent more time than I'll willingly admit debating the differences in colors, which honestly all looked the same to me. But I knew that getting it right was important to my partner, so I played along. The color we eventually chose literally looked exactly the same as the four we'd tried before, but I didn't complain. I was just happy to be out of those painting overalls.

Read books about pregnancy to get you clued up on what your partner is experiencing during each stage of pregnancy and what she may need. Help her make major decisions about the baby, such as which doctor to use or where to give birth. Attend birthing classes with her. Your physical presence by her side throughout this journey will help her more than you know.

Use Your Words

If you don't know, just ask! Communicating with your partner about what she needs and how best you can help her will make things a lot easier. Share your feelings with her and allow her to do the same. She's going through a lot, and lending her an ear will help her relieve a lot of her stress and anxiety.

Even if there's nothing you can do to help her in a specific situation, allow her to get whatever she needs off her chest. And don't be closed off either. If you're feeling scared or anxious, share those feelings with her. She's probably feeling the same way.

Remember, you're going through this experience together, so who better to lean on for support than each other?

And don't be afraid to reach out if you have friends who've recently had children. Ask them for advice on how to handle situations, or use them as a sounding board for your own ideas and opinions.

Physical Support During Pregnancy

Aside from the emotional rollercoaster that pregnancy straps you both into without warning, there's also the more obvious aspect of your partner's new physical limitations. Offering the right amount of physical support during her pregnancy will help ensure both her health and that of your unborn child. The physical support you give her will allow her to spend all her energy on the mammoth task of growing a human inside her.

Be the Change

Pregnancy will place a lot of restrictions on your partner, and some of them might be rather unpleasant. Why not take the plunge and join her? If she's quite partial to a quiet glass of wine in the evenings, she might find the loss of this small comfort rather upsetting. You could consider forgoing liquor in solidarity for the time being. Or maybe just allow yourself to have the occasional beer with the boys every now and then.

When she has to sacrifice things she enjoys for the sake of the baby, and you're still out there living your best life, she might start feeling a bit miffed, which is understandable. If you want to be supportive, be on her side with these changes. Adopting healthier eating habits as a couple will make it easier for her to adjust to her new dietary requirements as well. I know my partner was left with a sour taste in her mouth when she had to deprive herself of all the treats she used to enjoy, and I just went about my life as if I were oblivious. I knew she was doing it for the baby and that, in essence, she was doing it for me as well. I eventually sucked it up and hopped on the bandwagon.

It actually became a pretty fun exercise, completely overhauling our diets to make room for these new healthy habits. I also knew that it would be easier for her to resist the temptation of junk food if there wasn't any in the house. Sometimes, being a cheerleader on the sidelines while chugging a beer isn't enough encouragement. Being in this together meant we literally had to be in this together, and I wanted to do everything I could to make the pregnancy easier for her.

Be Hands-On

With her energy levels taking a nosedive and her mobility also on the decline, it was time for me to step up around the house and start doing more chores. It will take a load off her back if you take over doing the daily house cleaning so she can rest. You can start small by just offering to do things that you can see she hasn't gotten around to. But eventually, you'll probably end up doing most of it.

I don't think I really appreciated everything my partner did to keep our home clean until I was tasked with that duty. I couldn't believe how quickly dirty dishes can pile up in the sink! And how is there *always* dirty laundry? It was an eye-opening experience. Hey, outsource if you need to! Many amazing cleaning services won't charge you an arm and a leg to keep your home looking spotless. The point is to give your partner time to put her feet up and relax.

Be Nurturing

At this moment, indulge and pamper your partner to an unprecedented degree. Dim the lights, light some candles, and give her a nice back massage. Wrap her up in blankets on the couch and queue up all her favorite shows on Netflix. Make sure she really knows how much you appreciate her and admire her for carrying your child.

Especially on days when the pregnancy symptoms make her feel a little worse for wear, make an effort to do things that will make her day a little better. Buy her flowers, for no reason, serenade her with her favorite song. Sometimes, the little things will make the biggest difference in her day. Tell her she looks beautiful even when she's feeling bloated and under the weather. Obviously, you should make an effort to indulge your partner at every stage of your relationship; however, she will be particularly in need of it during her pregnancy.

Maintaining the Relationship

When there's a baby on the way, sometimes it becomes the center of your life. The pregnancy and the baby become all you can think about or talk about, and every conversation either begins or ends with them. However, you must continue putting effort into your relationship with your partner during this time. Continuing to strengthen and nurture your connection will put you in a better position to be a good parent. Aside from that, these are the last few months you'll have with just the two of you, so make them count! Once there's a baby in the mix, finding time to spend alone together will become so much more difficult. So make sure you take advantage of this opportunity to spend as much quality time with your partner as you can.

Keep the Romance Alive

As much as planning and preparing for your baby's arrival takes up most of your time, that shouldn't be all you and your partner are doing. Take the time to go on dates and do things together as a couple that have nothing to do with the pregnancy. Be spontaneous with gestures of your love for your partner, like buying her flowers randomly or stopping by her favorite bakery on your way home from work.

Remind her that you love her as often as possible, and sneak in all the kisses and cuddles you can. Go to the movies and hold hands, take a long romantic moonlit walk, and plan a candlelit dinner. Don't neglect your relationship. Remember, the kids will eventually grow up and move out to start their own lives; your partner is in it for the long haul. Make sure your relationship with each other is strong enough to make it all the way.

Be a Team

The best way to nurture your relationship during pregnancy is to make major decisions together. Discuss things with each other and make sure you're both involved with every step along the way. Being on the same page about important things will do wonders for your relationship.

Be prepared for disagreements, but don't take things too personally. When it comes to things like talking about parenting styles or instilling values, you might learn things about your partner that you didn't know. And you might not like some of those things. Use these differences as an opportunity to grow and gain a deeper understanding of each other; don't allow them to cause a rift between you. Talking openly and honestly with each other about your feelings is what will get you through some of the toughest times ahead. Foster that form of open communication now.

Make Time for Intimacy

When it comes to intimacy, sometimes pregnancy can make that difficult. Your sex life will depend on both your individual comfort levels and the status of your partner's pregnancy. Have that conversation. If the pregnancy is high-risk, your doctors might suggest you abstain from sexual activity. But remember that there are many ways to be intimate that don't involve having sex.

Be aware that the hormonal and physical changes that your partner undergoes during pregnancy will probably affect her sex drive. If she's feeling nauseous and bloated or has heartburn, of course, sex will be the furthest thing from her mind! Her changing body might also be making her feel insecure and not sexy, so be sensitive to that. With her growing belly getting in the way, you'll also probably need to get more inventive when it comes to comfortable positions in which to have sex.

Keeping that flame alive is important, and many couples neglect it in the face of all the stress and chaos of preparing for the baby. But if you can't find time for it now, you definitely won't find time for it after the baby is born. Your intimate connection with your partner is an important aspect of your relationship, and personal connection to each other.

Talk About the Future

Have you thought about your growing family? Have you discussed your expectations and shared your fears and anxieties? These are important conversations to have with your partner during pregnancy. Maybe you're not clear about each other's visions for the future, or you're unsure of your financial situation. Make sure that you're both on the same page when it comes to how you see the years unfolding. How do you plan on working out your family dynamic and the possibility of growing your family even further?

Knowing that you have created a vision for the future together that you're both happy with and can prepare for will be both comforting and reassuring for you as a couple.

Deepening your emotional connection to your partner during pregnancy is an important foundation on which to build your future as a parent. Remember, a child is a physical manifestation of your love for each other, so make sure that you keep that love alive! Supporting your partner through the pregnancy means knowing how to handle the rollercoaster of emotions that she's on without feeding into it. Find ways to be her refuge in the hormonal storm. If you can learn how to help her get through some of the more turbulent emotional outbursts, you'll make the journey through pregnancy a lot more enjoyable for both of you.

Being supportive during pregnancy is about more than just offering a shoulder to lean on; it's about getting involved and being hands-on. Take the initiative to learn more about pregnancy and read up on what's happening in her body. Be present for her throughout this experience by attending scans with her and signing up for prenatal classes as a couple. Be a part of preparing for the baby, building the nursery, and buying essential items in preparation for the baby's arrival.

In all the chaos, don't forget to continue nurturing the connection you have with your partner. Maintaining your relationship is important because, if you don't make an effort to spend quality time together now, you'll be less likely to as your family grows. Continue to fan that flame of intimacy and romance, and don't neglect to express the love and appreciation you have for each other. A family is built on the foundation of the love that exists between you and your partner, so keep that foundation strong!

Now that we know all about what's happening in your partner's belly and we've built a firm foundation from which to spring into this new journey of parenthood, it's time to get down to the nitty-gritty. What are the practical preparations you need to make for the baby's arrival? Let's dive into that in the next chapter.

3

PLANNING AND PREPARING FOR PARENTHOOD

I came to parenting the way most of us do — knowing nothing and trying to learn everything.

— MAYIM BIALIK

SOMEONE ONCE TOLD me that if you wait until you can afford to have a child, you'll never end up having one. This is true in so many ways. You've probably spent countless sleepless nights sitting up crunching numbers, trying to figure out how you're going to make it work. Trust me, I've been there. The weird thing about parenthood is that, somehow, it does work itself out. I'm not saying to cast your financial future up to the gods and hope for the best, but there's a point at which you need to accept that your finances are going to be a stress point from here on out. Yet, somehow, parents still make it work. In this chapter, we'll be tackling the major questions you probably have about preparing for the baby. And we're not just talking about money.

You've probably heard of baby-proofing by now, and you're wondering how to turn your home into an oasis of safety for your upcoming bundle of joy. From socket safety plugs to corner guards for your tables, we'll be dissecting all the little ways you'll need to protect your home from those tiny, exploring fingers and curious eyes.

I'll also be giving you the low-down on some of those things your partner's always going on about that you still have no clue what they mean, like birthing plans. And what exactly is supposed to go into the hospital bag anyway? Isn't she just supposed to give birth and come home? Why does she need luggage? I'll be answering all these questions and more. By the end of this chapter, you'll feel more than ready to bring that baby home.

Baby on a Budget

Let's start with the elephant in the room: finances. No doubt, adding a new mouth to feed your household will have massive financial implications. A lot of the costs involved with having a baby are, thankfully, once-off. This will include things like buying a cot, car seat, feeding chair, and other necessary items for their care. After that, you'll need to start considering their monthly needs, like childcare, diapers, formula, and clothes. Yes, clothes. They outgrow them faster than you can believe! And, of course, let's not forget about healthcare.

When you're sitting down to prepare your baby's budget, you need to start by considering what your financial priorities are. Of course, you'll want to start saving up for your child's education, but that's not really advisable. What you should rather focus on for the time being is putting some money away in a rainy-day fund, paying off any toxic debts you may have, and making sure you'll be taken care of when you retire.

This might not feel intuitively right, but you'll be setting yourself up for a better financial outlook if you plan your finances this way.

Live Below Your Means

Babies don't have a lot of financial needs in those first few years, so the bigger source of financial stress might be a change in your income. In cases where one parent is going to stop working, there will obviously be major financial implications. Factor that when you're preparing your baby's budget,

Suppose you can start learning how to manage the reduced income before the baby arrives. Work out ways that you can make that budget work, and put their salary towards that rainy day fund.

Be Flexible

The expenses involved in raising a child are forever changing. As one expense becomes redundant, another will take its place, so you need to learn to be flexible.

Have the foresight to start preparing for an additional expense well in advance so you're not left in a lurch. For example, after a few years, things like diapers and formula will no longer be an expense. However, new costs like those for extracurricular activities and school fees will take their place, so try to budget ahead.

There's no fixed amount that you can plan to put towards your child for the rest of their life, so make sure you're able to adapt your budget to their changing needs. The better you become at anticipating changing expenses, the easier it will be to adjust through the transition.

Always Have a Plan B

No matter how well you try and plan for your financial future, there may inevitably come a time when you fall short. Don't panic; these things happen. What's important is that you have contingencies in place for when this happens.

Some good fallback options for when the funds dry up are:

- Skimping on unnecessary monthly subscriptions
- Finding a side hustle to bring in some extra cash on the side
- Refinancing your mortgage
- Trading in your car for a cheaper one

Birth Plans

I had no idea that birth plans existed before my partner got pregnant. Why would I? In the movies, giving birth always looks like something that happens when you least expect it. There's the sudden breaking of her water, the mad rush to the hospital, and then, in a split second, a baby pops out. Nothing in that scenario seems planned to me! Thankfully, I know better now. I spent hours discussing birth options with my partner, and it turns out that giving birth is quite the occasion.

If you're lost at sea like I was, allow me to shed some light. A birth plan is the sequence of events your partner would like to have unfolded on the day of her delivery. It includes things like where she wants to give birth and how she wants to give birth. Most women have an idea in their minds of how they want this beautiful experience to happen, down to the most minute detail! However, it's also important to remember that a birth plan is not set in stone, and sometimes changes, need to be made on the day. For example, your partner might insist that she wants to go completely natural, only to realize on the day that it hurts a lot more than she anticipated, and she might just need something to take the edge off. It's not in your best interest to refuse her this request simply because it wasn't part of her birth plan.

The first consideration for your birth plan is where your partner wants to give birth. Generally, her options are:

- At a hospital
- At a birthing center
- At home

These options all have their own merits for various reasons, and her choice will depend mostly on what her priorities are.

Hospital Birth

If safety is her primary concern, then hospitals are your best bet. A hospital will give you immediate access to necessary medical personnel in the event of an emergency. She would also be able to receive pain relief there and have the option of a caesarean section if need be. Some people find the sterile environment of hospitals to be too impersonal and aren't comfortable with the endless foot traffic wandering in and out of the room during labor.

Birthing Center

If your partner is looking for more homely, private labor and delivery, she might want to consider a birthing center. A birthing center has the added benefit of offering a wider variety of birthing options, like a water birth. A birthing center is only an option if your partner wants a natural birth, however, as they don't have the medical facilities for a caesarean. For those wanting to give birth with as little medical intervention as possible, a birthing center is a great option. It has a very comforting environment while still giving you access to medical personnel. However, birthing centers are only an option if your partner has a low-risk pregnancy and wants to give birth vaginally without pain medication.

Home Birth

If your partner wants complete autonomy over her labor and birth experience, she might choose to give birth at home. Although a midwife will be present, a home birth gives your partner the freedom to decide how she wants to handle her labor without being bound by hospital policies or external pressures. Giving birth at home will also probably make your partner feel a lot more comfortable and relaxed during labor, resulting in a much less stressful birth experience. The risk of home birth is that, should a medical emergency arise, there won't be doctors on hand to immediately intervene. It's also a far less sterile environment than a birthing center or hospital, leading to an increased risk of infection.

As you can see, every birthing option has its merits and risks. It's up to you and your partner to weigh the pros and cons and decide which option will work best for you.

In addition to where she will give birth, a birth plan will also specify who she wants in the room during the birth and the position she'd like to give birth in if she wants things like dim lights or music playing during labor. Essentially, a birth plan lets everyone involved know the ideal scenario your partner envisions for her labor and delivery. But always remember to remain flexible and, much like in the movies, birth can be unpredictable.

Preparing for the New Arrival

Now that we've addressed the necessary planning you can do ahead of the big day let's get our hands dirty with some practical preparations. You've probably had dozens of interest boards with pictures of nurseries shoved in your face, but a nursery is more than just aesthetic. It's cute to look at wallpapers covered in bunnies or hanging lights shaped like helicopters, but what are some of the essential items that a good nursery should include? Let's take a look.

The Nursery

Seeing as your baby will spend the majority of their first few weeks in the nursery, it's probably the room you'll want to focus the most on at first. How you choose to decorate it is up to you, but what goes inside is more important. Essentially, a nursery needs to include four things:

1. a crib
2. a changing table or station
3. a dresser
4. a chair

Everything else is just frills. As long as these four pieces of furniture are in place, you're good to go. When choosing pieces of furniture for the nursery, it's important to consider durability and versatility. For example, certain cribs are able to be converted into toddler beds, data beds, and even double beds. Thinking long-term, this would be a wise purchase because you'd be able to keep it on for a long time, and it will grow with your child. There are also changing stations that convert into dressers for longer usability. Buying items that can be adapted to suit your baby's changing needs is a good investment.

The placement of the furniture is also important, and not just because of the Instagram pics, but for practicality. For instance, you don't want the crib to be in a position where the morning sun will blind your child. Situating the crib near outside walls might also be ill-advised due to changing temperatures. These are all minor things to take into consideration when planning your nursery.

Another thing you need to consider is lighting. Having multiple sources of lighting is a good idea because those overhead lights can be quite harsh, although installing a dimmer is always an option. Putting a lamp beside the chair where your partner will be nursing the baby will be helpful for those late-night feedings. Night lights are a fun and easy way to keep babies calm and entertained as they drift off to sleep and add a nice touch to the room.

The fun part of preparing your nursery is choosing the theme and decorations. Be careful not to go too overboard, because if the room is too stimulating, your baby might not be able to sleep. Choose calm, soothing colors; you can always redecorate as your child gets older. Blackout curtains will ensure your baby's sleep isn't interrupted by things like streetlights or the neighbor's motion-sensor porch light.

If you'd like a little peace of mind, you can also get a baby monitor. That way, you can continue with your day while the baby sleeps and still keep a watchful eye on them.

Baby-Proofing

As much as we wish we could keep the baby safe and confined to the nursery, soon your little bundle of joy will be mobile and wanting to explore the rest of the house. When that time comes, you'll feel less anxious knowing that any potential hazards have already been taken care of. Baby-proofing the house is about anticipating any potential catastrophes and making necessary alterations to prevent them from happening.

That being said, you'd be surprised at how crafty and cunning those little hands can be, and they'll probably still find ways to cause chaos despite your best efforts. If there are spaces that you don't feel like you can make entirely safe for your little explorer, you can simply block access to those rooms using a baby security gate. Installing these gates at the tops and bottoms of stairs is a good place to start as well.

Baby-proofing isn't a once-off task, and you'll probably need to keep updating your security measures as your baby grows and develops new skills and is able to reach more things.

Here are some of the basics to get you started:

- Put safety covers over all of your electrical outlets.
- Remove any curtains or blinds with dangling cords that your baby can reach up and grab, or install a hook around which you can wrap those cords.
- Hide any cables or tape them down.
- Get baby-safe latches for all your cupboards and drawers to prevent your baby from accidentally shutting them on their fingers.
- Install non-slip pads underneath all of your rugs and carpets.
- Anchor all your furniture to prevent your baby from tipping anything over onto themselves.
- Lock any dangerous items away in a cupboard the baby can't reach.
- Cover the sharp edges of all your furniture with padding.

If you want to get a better understanding of what needs to be baby-proofed, try looking at your house from your child's perspective. Yes, I mean, get down on your hands and knees and crawl around. It will be so much easier to spot any potential temptation from this point of view. I had no idea how many choking hazards there were in my living room until I started baby-proofing. Not sure what constitutes a choking hazard? Try the toilet roll trick.

Using a toilet roll is a great way to test for choking hazards. Anything that you can fit into the center of the toilet roll is a choking hazard and should be kept out of reach. Babies are naturally curious and have an odd habit of putting anything they find into their mouths. The best way to avoid unnecessary trips to the ER is to limit their access to anything that could potentially harm them.

What's in the Bag?

I was so baffled when our midwife kept reminding me to prepare the hospital bag and keep it in my car for the final weeks of pregnancy. I had no idea what that was or what it entailed. I assumed my partner would give birth, take a nap, then come straight home. Yes, I know, I was in for a shock. Anyway, if you too are at a loss as to what this mythical hospital bag is: It's a bag containing all the essential items your partner will need for labor and delivery. Normally, the hospital or birthing center can provide you with a list of what to include if you ask. Depending on the birthing plan your partner opts for, she might have a few items that she wants included. In general, however, a hospital bag should include the following items:

- a pair of non-slip socks
- a dressing gown

- a clean pair of pajamas
- bottled water
- glucose/snacks (labor can be *long*)
- phone charger
- important paperwork like your healthcare information or documents needed for birth registration
- an outfit for your baby to come home in
- a pillow
- a comfortable set of clothing for your partner to wear when she leaves to go home
- basic toiletries
- maternity pads
- nappies/diapers
- wet wipes
- breast pads
- things to entertain yourself with: books, magazines, playing cards etc.

Remember that giving birth isn't like in the movies, where she labors for a few minutes, and then a baby pops out. It can be an incredibly long process, so make sure you've bought things to keep yourself busy during that time. But not so much that you forget why you're there.

Preparing Your Relationship

As important as it is for you to make sure your home is ready to receive your baby, it's not just the house that needs prepping. You also need to prepare your relationship for this new addition. So many couples get overwhelmed in those early months because they didn't put enough thought into the oncoming changes and how they would affect their relationship. Taking some time to plan ahead for how you'll both adjust and settle into parenting is a great way to avoid clashing over small things down the line.

Share Your Expectations

You probably both have ideas in your minds about the kinds of parents you want to be, but have you shared those ideas? You both need to be on the same page concerning your new roles and the expectations you've placed on yourselves and each other. You should both be aware of how you'd like to fulfill your parenting roles and then give each other the space to do that. On top of figuring out how you're each going to adjust to being a parent, you also need to make sure you're working together as a team.

Share the Workload

You'd be surprised how tense it can get in the household after a few weeks with a screaming newborn. You're both exhausted and feeling overworked. Start planning how to divvy up baby responsibilities now while you're still able to do so in a calm and level-headed way. It's far more frustrating to try and figure it out down the line when it's 3 a.m., and your partner is claiming that you haven't done your fair share of diaper changes for the day. Remember, being a team isn't about pointing fingers at each other or keeping track of who's doing more work or who's sacrificing more sleep. Work out a system well in advance on how you're going to share the load, and don't forget to allot some time off occasionally. You'll need it!

Take Shifts at Night

Sleep deprivation has become almost synonymous with caring for a newborn. The fact that they need to be fed every two hours should already tell you that you won't be getting your full 8 hours for some time. However, that doesn't mean that you need to get so little sleep that you're unable to function the next day. Between your partner and yourself, do your best to split night wakings and feedings in such a way that you can both still get a decent chunk of sleep. Split the evenings into shifts instead of taking turns. That way, you can get a longer stretch of sleep in between. Alternating nights is a terrible idea; trust me, I tried it. Some nights, the baby is easier than others; it's better to work it out so that you're both contributing. There's nothing worse than spending all night with a screaming baby while your partner slumbers obliviously because it's not their turn.

Having these conversations before the baby is born will prevent them from becoming sources of conflict later on. The stress of looking after a newborn is already quite overwhelming; there's no need to add relationship stress to that as well.

Planning for the future can go a long way toward easing some of the stress and anxiety you're feeling in anticipation of your child's arrival. As a dad, one of your main concerns is probably how you're going to financially cope with adding a new mouth to feed. Thankfully, you can start preparing yourself during pregnancy for the oncoming expenses you can expect. Having a rainy day fund will help you feel less panicked when things don't go quite as planned. Remember to stay flexible, because life is unpredictable and things can and will happen.

As much as a birthing plan is something your partner may feel they have the ultimate decision on, you can still play an important role in making that decision. Depending on what her priorities are and what kind of birth experience she wants, there are many options available. Help her weigh the pros and cons of each option before making a decision, and remember that a birth plan is just that: a plan. It's not set in stone, and ultimately, things might not end up going that way.

Preparing your home for a baby is no mean feat. Baby-proofing might leave your home looking completely different than when you started, but you can never be too safe. Babies are endlessly curious, and they move faster than you can believe. When getting the nursery ready, make sure it's practical and not just Instagram-worthy. Allow your partner to decorate to her heart's content as long as the essentials are in place.

Packing a hospital bag a few weeks in advance will save you from forgetting important things in the mad rush to get to the hospital or birthing center. Keep it in your car for that final stretch of pregnancy so you at least know it's there when you need it.

Preparing for your baby isn't just about creating a budget and installing security gates around the stairs, it's also about preparing your relationship. The mental toll that adding a newborn to the household can take on both you and your partner can lead to unnecessary turmoil within your relationship. You can avoid unnecessary conflicts by discussing important adjustments before the baby arrives. At least that way, you both know you're on the same page and are embarking on your parenting journey as a team.

Now that you've prepared yourself, your home, and your relationship for the arrival of your baby, let's talk more about the arrival itself. Childbirth is a transformative experience, and not just for your partner. You're probably anxious about what you can expect on the big day and what will be expected of you. Let's take a deep breath together and dive into childbirth in the next chapter.

PART II

THE CHILDBIRTH EXPERIENCE

4

PREPARING YOURSELF FOR CHILDBIRTH

Death, taxes, and childbirth! There's never any convenient time for any of them.

— MARGARET MITCHELL

YOU'VE PROBABLY TRIED to picture your child so many times in your mind by now, but it comes up blank. Sometimes, even our imaginations can't fathom the incredible miracle that lies ahead. The same can probably be said of the birth experience itself. Try as you may, you can't imagine what it will be like. And you know what? You probably won't be able to describe it afterward, either. Witnessing the birth of your child is such a uniquely intense event. It's one of those things you can only understand if you've experienced it for yourself. But that doesn't mean you can't prepare for it, because you definitely should. The pregnancy journey has probably been such a rollercoaster of overwhelming emotions for you already that you wouldn't even know where to begin getting ready for the actual birth. All of this has led up to this one moment, and that can leave you feeling both terrified and excited. In this chapter, we'll look at ways you can prepare yourself for that penultimate moment. The moment you meet your child for the first time. The day you become a father.

Understanding the Emotional Rollercoaster

Just because your partner is the one carrying the baby doesn't mean you're any less affected by the intense emotions that come along with pregnancy. The prospect of becoming a parent is daunting for anyone, and you may often be wrestling with your emotions.

It's normal to experience periods of fear and anxiety. After all, your life is about to change. Any major transition in life can bring up feelings of fear. You might be questioning whether or not you'll be a good parent, or you might be worried about the health of your partner and your unborn child. You might be stressed about how you're going to cope financially with the costs involved with raising a child. Maybe you're scared because you don't know if you're ready to take on such a massive responsibility. All of these feelings are completely valid, so don't beat yourself up over having them.

Of course, it's not all doom and gloom either. You'll find yourself getting more and more excited as the date approaches, itching to finally meet your child. Sometimes, it's like you can't sit still because you're so ablaze with anticipation! This is normal, too. Becoming a father is such an incredible experience. You're probably already picturing all of the amazing things you're going to do with your child. All of the fun adventures you're going to take them on.

If you find yourself obsessively worrying about the birth itself, you're not alone there either. Some soon-to-be fathers suffer from a paralyzing fear of childbirth. This can be caused by many factors, such as not really knowing much about what giving birth entails or being unsure of the role you'll be playing during that process. The role that a father plays during childbirth has come a very long way. A hundred years ago, you wouldn't even be allowed to set foot in the maternity ward. These days, however, fathers are permitted to play a much more hands-on role during childbirth. You get to stay by your partner's side and support her right to the very end if you want to.

Maybe you're on edge because you're not sure if you want to be in the room at all. Or maybe you're feeling just a bit too much pressure to be around for the birth, and you're not quite sure if you can handle it. Hey, I get it. Seeing your partner in that much pain won't be easy. And who knows how you'd even react in a situation like that? What if you do something embarrassing, like faint? Trust me, you wouldn't be the first! Those doctors really have seen it all. Preparing for the birth emotionally is also about understanding your own limitations and accepting what you can or cannot handle.

The best way you can process these feelings is not to bottle them up or try to ignore or suppress them. Talk to someone about them; get them out of your head. Lay your cards out on the table with your partner and see what their views are. Chances are, they've been feeling the same way. Maybe they're not quite sure how to bring up the topic with you and are also uncertain of what your wishes are regarding the actual birth. Sure, they're the ones giving birth, but this is also about you. It's your child, too.

Don't judge yourself for feeling a certain way about things or feel guilty for not feeling a certain way. This is unchartered territory for both of you, so remember that all of your feelings are valid. You might even find that your views and feelings change as the pregnancy progresses. Perhaps right now, you can't even fathom wanting to be there when she gives birth, but closer to the time, you get so excited that you simply can't miss it! Allow yourself to go with your feelings and be true to yourself about what makes you comfortable.

Getting Ready for the Big Day

The mental preparation for childbirth can be quite a laborious task and perhaps not one you'll ever fully feel like you've completed. Remember that it's a process that you need to follow through and see where it takes you. The physical preparations you can do for the big day are a lot more simple.

As a father, I know I always feel a lot more useful when I'm actively preparing for something. That way, I can at least measure and track my progress and feel some sort of accomplishment.

Preparing for childbirth as a dad can be tricky because it's different depending on your situation. Start by thoroughly considering the role you'd like to play on the day. How involved would you like to be in the birthing process? How involved would your partner like you to be? Having an open and honest conversation with your partner regarding her expectations is not only important but will also help you know how best to get ready for the big day.

Let's look at some of the best ways you can prepare for childbirth:

Educate Yourself

Doing research into labor and delivery will help you understand what you can expect. Get a better understanding of what labor entails so you can know how best to support your partner throughout that process. Attending a childbirth class is also a great way to familiarize yourself with labor and delivery. It's also a good opportunity for you to meet and connect with other expecting parents so that you can share your experience. Having other people in your life who are traveling along the same journey will help you feel more at ease and confident going into the experience.

Make Arrangements Early

Prepare well ahead of time for all the necessary arrangements that need to be made for the day. This includes things like organizing someone to look after your pets and making a list of people you and your partner would like to contact regarding the birth announcement.

Set the Mood

Have a conversation with your partner beforehand about what kind of music she'd like to be played during labor and delivery. You can even sit down and create a playlist together. Make sure you know if she wants any specific candles or incense to be burned unless of course you're in a hospital which will prohibit the burning of *anything*. Familiarize yourself with all the minor details she'd like to have included in her birthing experience and do your best to make them a reality.

Get Friendly With Her Team

Take a tour of the facility where your partner intends to give birth and familiarize yourself with it. Get to know the medical personnel on her team, such as her nurses, OBGYN, midwife, and doula. Forming a relationship with these vital people will make the birthing experience more pleasant and make it easier for you to communicate with each other regarding how best to support your partner through labor on the day.

Know Your Partner's Wishes

Study your partner's birth plan thoroughly, so you're properly clued up on what she wants. She might be too distracted on the day to express her wishes, so it's going to be up to you to be her advocate. Don't be afraid to be firm with the midwife or nurses when it comes to honoring your partner's wishes, but remember to be flexible. Things won't always go exactly according to plan.

Playing Your Part

One of the biggest concerns you may have is your involvement in the labor and delivery process. Discussing this with your partner is the best way to quell some of these anxieties. You should come to an agreement that both allows your partner to get the level of support that she needs but also respects the level of involvement that you'd be comfortable with.

There are four main types of support that you could offer your partner during the day. Let's look at them below:

The Coach

This is the most involved role a dad can play in labor and delivery. Being her coach means being right by her side every step of the way. You'll help guide your partner through their contractions, reminding them to do their breathing exercises. You'll also assist her with getting into the various labor positions she's chosen and be there to rub and massage her back during labor. As her coach, you'll be the one to advocate for your partner's wishes with regard to the birth plan and do your best to ensure things go as close to the way she wants as possible. You might even get the opportunity to lift the baby onto her stomach after it has been delivered.

You might also choose to share the role of being her coach with a close friend or family member, like your partner's mother. Labor can be an incredibly long process and you may need to take breaks in between. It will help to know that your partner isn't left alone during those times.

The Teammate

If you're not really comfortable taking on such a hands-on role during the birth, you might want to only be partially involved. As a teammate, you'd be there to help your partner as much as you could but leave the majority of the support to someone else. You'd be there to help out and provide support when needed, but other than that, take a bit more of a backseat.

In this case, it might be advisable for your partner to also hire a doula. A doula is basically a non-medical professional who provides women with physical and emotional support during labor. The doula would then play the role of advocate on behalf of your partner and be the one to help guide them through contractions and breathing meditations.

The Spectator

This is the most commonly chosen option for dads. As much as you want to be there to support your partner, you'd rather cheer them on from the sidelines than be hands-on. And that's okay! Being there to rub their back and encourage them through labor is just as vital and beneficial for your partner. You could even play cameraman and capture the amazing moments leading up to the birth, possibly even the birth itself. You may even cut the umbilical cord. Being a spectator doesn't mean you're not involved; it just means you'd rather leave the finer details to the professionals.

On the Bench

In some cases, for whatever reason, you and your partner might decide that it's best for you not to be in the room during the birth and rather wait elsewhere. There's no shame in this either. Remember, there's no right or wrong way to support your partner through labor; there's just the way that works best for you.

Be In It Together

Imagine you came home one day, and your partner had already chosen a name for the baby without any input from you. How would that make you feel? Probably more than a little hurt.

A lot of fathers struggle with feeling like they're not part of the pregnancy. Of course, so much attention is given to your partner because they're the ones carrying the child. It's so much easier for them to understand their role in the pregnancy and to build a strong connection with the baby before it is born. For you, it's a lot more difficult. Without making a concerted effort, you might just begin to feel like this pregnancy doesn't include you at all.

One of the best ways for you to feel like you're playing a pivotal role in your partner's pregnancy journey, aside from actively attending doctor's appointments and prenatal classes with her, is for you to make all the major decisions together. By involving you in the process of making any decisions related to the baby, your partner will greatly improve your ability to feel included in the pregnancy journey.

Some major decisions you'll want to discuss with your partner include:

- picking the child's name
- creating a birth plan

- choosing a doctor or midwife
- decorating the nursery
- deciding when to announce the birth
- taking leave from work
- when or whether to find out the baby's gender
- who will be present at the birth

Learning how to work together to make important decisions as a couple during pregnancy will make it easier for you to parent together as a team going forward.

Childbirth is such a pivotal moment for both you and your partner. When gearing up for the big event, it's important to take your own feelings and thoughts into consideration. As much as you want to support your partner and be there for all of their needs, that doesn't mean you need to neglect your own. You're allowed to have boundaries, and don't be afraid to express them. This is essentially about both of you. Do as much as you feel comfortable doing, and don't feel pressured to overexert yourself because nobody will benefit in that scenario.

Being proactive in preparing for the big day will help you feel more confident when the time comes. Make sure you're aware of your partner's wishes for her birthing experience so you can help ensure she has what she needs. Also, it will be very helpful for you to take care of things like the hospital bag, informing relatives, packing snacks, bringing candles, etc., because she'll be far too distracted to remember those things on the day.

Leading up to the birth, you're going to go through an endless cycle of intense emotions, and that's okay. Everything you're feeling is valid; change can be scary. And becoming a parent is one of the biggest changes a person can go through. So be kind to yourself through this process and know that you're doing the best you can.

Now that you've got all your ducks in a row let's get down to the main event. In the next chapter, we'll be delving into what you can expect during labor and delivery.

5

EMBRACING THE CHILDBIRTH
JOURNEY—FROM LABOR TO
DELIVERY

Childbirth is more admirable than conquest, more amazing than self-defense, and as courageous as either one.

— GLORIA STEINEM

YOU PROBABLY FELT your heartbeat accelerate just from reading the title of this chapter. I know the feeling. I couldn't quite describe how I felt in those final days just before the birth. There were so many emotions running through me, and they were all so intense that sometimes I felt nauseous. I was both overwhelmed with excitement and paralyzed by fear. However, when the time finally comes, and your partner is officially in that final stretch, it's important to reign that all in so you can be the most effective support for her during labor and delivery. In this chapter, we'll break labor and delivery down into bite-size pieces for you to chew on while you eagerly wait for the big day.

In these cases, forewarned is forearmed. The process of childbirth is absolutely nothing like what you've seen on TV, so forget everything you think you know. Knowing what to expect will empower you to be at least aware of what your partner is experiencing and be prepared for what's coming next. The various stages of labor bring with them different challenges and various coping strategies you can use to guide your partner through them.

As a supportive partner, no matter how involved you plan to be, it will be helpful for you to be able to recognize the different stages of labor and be able to assist your partner with each transition. So get ready to strap those gloves on because we're diving right in!

First Stage of Labor

There are three stages of labor, and the first one is the longest. Unlike in the movies, giving birth doesn't happen instantaneously. Actually, for a first pregnancy, your partner might be in labor for hours or even days! This first stage occurs in three separate phases. The first of these is early labor.

Early Labor

Early labor, also known as the latent phase, is your signal that it's time to meet your baby! During the early phase of labor, your partner's cervix begins to thin out, also known as effacing. The cervix also starts to dilate in order to create an opening wide enough for the baby to be able to pass through.

Your partner's body goes about this through contractions. Contractions are the regular, rhythmic tightening and releasing of the muscles in her uterus, and yes, they hurt. A lot. The closer your partner gets to giving birth, the more frequent and intense her contractions will become. In early labor, however, the pain should be somewhat manageable.

It would be very helpful for you to be able to recognize the early signs of labor. Your partner might be in labor if she experiences any combination of the following:

- **Mild contractions**: Not to be confused with Braxton Hicks, labor contractions don't just feel like a tightening of her stomach but will actually cause her pain. The pain won't be too severe and will be comparable to menstrual cramping. Contractions during early labor are usually not consistent and can happen anywhere between five and 20 minutes apart.
- **Bloody show**: I know this sounds like something out of a Hitchcock film, but it's just the name given to describe the process of your partner losing their mucous plug. The mucous plug is what keeps the cervix sealed during pregnancy, and losing it is a clear sign that the pregnancy is now over. If your partner finds discharge in her underwear that's pink or bloody, she may have lost her mucous plug.
- **Water breaking**: If your partner experiences a trickle of liquid down her thighs, this might be a sign that her waters have broken. This water is the liquid in which your baby has been growing, and its release is a sign that the baby is ready to come out. No matter how far into labor your partner has progressed at that point, if her waters break, you need to either call her doctor immediately or take her to the hospital.

As we've stated, early labor is unpredictable and can last for any length of time. When it comes to first-time mothers, particularly, it can even drag on for days. For that reason, most doctors will recommend your partner stay at home through this first phase of labor. If you go into the hospital and they discover that your partner is less than 4 cm dilated, they'll probably send you home then as well.

They do this for a variety of reasons. Firstly, because they don't know if it could last days, but also because your partner will probably find early labor more comfortable at home. The length of her labor will depend on how relaxed and comfortable she is, so it's in both of your best interests that she remain as calm and tranquil as possible.

Early labor is the time for you to break out all of those items she requested on her birth plan. Light the scented candles or incense, dim the lights, and plug in the playlist. A happy mother is a calm mother, and both of those make for easier labor. Try to keep your partner as relaxed as possible during this time. Rub her back during her contractions and help her breathe her way through them.

Encourage her to do things, but nothing too hectic. She can watch her favorite movies, soak in a nice bath, or even take a nap if she likes. The most important thing to do in early labor is unwind and not put too much stress or pressure on her.

You can also help her by timing her contractions. Contractions are timed in minutes from the start of one to the start of the next one. There are also apps you can download that will help you track them. Make sure you're keeping in contact with her medical team throughout this process, giving them regular updates on the progress of her labor and any developments.

When your partner reaches a point where her contractions are five minutes apart or less, are longer than thirty seconds in duration, and continue adhering to those parameters for an hour, it's time to go to the hospital!

Active Labor

Active labor is when things get real. Your partner's contractions are no longer just mild and uncomfortable but are intense and severely painful. Maybe before, she could still focus and talk during her contractions, but during active labor, you'll be lucky to get much more than a grunt.

Labor will really start to pick up during this phase, and the contractions will continue to become longer with shorter intervals between them. At this point, your partner might request some form of pain relief. If she's chosen to have a drug-free labor, now would be the time to break out all those breathing exercises and relaxation techniques you learned during your birthing classes.

Finding comfortable positions will become increasingly difficult as labor progresses from this point. Thankfully, the active phase of labor isn't nearly as long as the latent phase and will probably be between four and eight hours, sometimes a little more. During this phase, her cervix will likely dilate 1 cm per hour.

Transition

Transition is the final phase of the first stage of labor and, by all accounts, the worst. During the transition, your partner will experience the most intense levels of pain associated with labor. Contractions will probably feel like they're happening one right after the other and will last up to 90 seconds each.

During the transition, your partner will feel a strong pressure in her rectum and might start having a very strong urge to push. Thankfully, the transition usually only lasts for 15 minutes to an hour.

The Second Stage of Labor

The second stage of labor begins when your cervix has dilated to 10 cm, and your baby has begun the descent into your partner's birth canal and emergence into the world!

As soon as your partner starts pushing, her contractions will become less intense and less frequent. Your partner's body will tell her when she needs to push, with intervals of rest in between. These contractions won't be widening her cervix but rather pushing your baby further down the birth canal. If your partner has elected to have an epidural, she might not really be able to feel the urge to push. In these cases, her doctor will guide her and let her know when she needs to push.

Soon, the skin joining her anus to her vagina, known as the perineum, will start to bulge out every time she pushes. That's how you'll know that the baby is getting closer. Shortly thereafter, your baby's scalp will become visible. This beautiful moment is known as crowning. We say the baby is *crowned* when the widest part of its head has become visible. At this point, your partner will experience a searing, sharp, stinging sensation, referred to as *the ring of fire*. I'm sure you can imagine why.

To make it easier to birth the baby, the doctor might cut your partner's perineum. This will help the vagina open wider as the baby comes out and is known as an episiotomy. Once the baby's head is out, its body will rotate inside your partner's pelvis to make for a smoother exit. Your baby will start to emerge with the following push, one shoulder at a time, then the rest of their body.

The moment you lay eyes on your child for the first time is not something I can ever explain to you. Even fresh out of the womb and covered in all manner of fluids, they will still be the most beautiful thing you've ever seen. Depending on your partner's wishes, the doctor might place the baby immediately on her chest or clean them off a little first and empty their nasal passages with a suction tool if they appear to have a lot of mucous.

You might find yourself overcome with a wave of unparalleled emotions. Joy, relief, amazement, awe, shock. You might even surprise yourself with your reaction; I know I certainly did. I both laughed and cried simultaneously at the birth of my first child. I'd never cried such tears of joy before, and it was a moment that I will never forget.

If you've elected to cut the umbilical cord, now is your time to shine! The doctor will clamp the cord, hand you a pair of surgical scissors, and show you where you need to cut.

The second stage of labor can take anywhere from 15 minutes to several hours, depending on a variety of factors. If this is your partner's first child, it will probably take longer. Should your child need to adjust themselves for a smoother delivery, this might also make the process longer.

The Third Stage of Labor

You might be so swept up in all the emotions you feel regarding the birth of your child that you'll forget the labor isn't over yet. The third stage of labor is when your partner delivers the placenta. The placenta is the sac your baby has been living in for the last nine months.

Your partner will experience mild contractions as her body prepares to deliver both the placenta and the membranes attached to it. This usually happens within 30 minutes of your partner giving birth. Once delivered, the doctor will inspect the placenta to ensure that it's still intact. No remnants of the placenta or membranes must remain inside your partner, as this could lead to infections.

After delivering the placenta, your partner will continue to experience mild contractions for some time as her uterus prepares to return to its normal size. During the time immediately following the birth, the doctor will make sure any damage suffered during the birth is repaired, including stitching up any tears. Your baby will be weighed, cleaned, and wrapped in a blanket for warmth, and your partner will be allowed to begin breastfeeding if she so wishes.

The process of labor can be both brutal and beautiful. Depending on how and where your partner decides to give birth and how involved you choose to be, you may experience any number of variations of this labor and delivery journey. What's important is that you are aware of what labor entails and how best you can support your partner through each of the stages. Seeing my partner give birth forever changed the way I viewed her. I gained a new level of reverence and respect for her—not that I didn't respect her before, I had just never stopped to appreciate how much pain and distress women went through while giving birth. I mean, I'd never be able to do it. It also gave me a newfound appreciation for my own mother, now that I have witnessed what she must have had to go through to have me.

But obviously, the most transformative aspect of the labor and birth experience was witnessing the birth of my child. It felt like the culmination of so much stress, fear, and anxiety. The previous nine months were at the forefront of my mind and all my partner and I had been through and had to overcome to finally find ourselves at that moment. I thought of all the discussions and arguments, all the excitement and anticipation. All of that melts away when you look into that tiny face for the first time. I also felt such an overwhelming sense of responsibility. I looked into my child's face and immediately knew I would do everything in my power to love and protect them and that I would work my fingers to the bone to ensure I could give them the best life possible.

It's a lot to place on one single moment, but it's a turning point in any man's life—becoming a father. I can tell you now that, even if you're exhausted after an incredibly long and exhausting labor, even if your nerves are shot and you can't feel your fingers because your partner has been squeezing them so hard, even if you feel like you're about to pass out and you're starving and sorry you missed out on that morning cup of coffee, even with all of that going on, you will look into that little face and know, in the deepest depths of your heart, that it was all worth it.

6

POST-DELIVERY—THE FIRST STEPS
INTO PARENTHOOD

*The guys who fear becoming fathers don't understand that fathering is
not something perfect men do, but something that perfects the man. The
end product of child-raising is not the child but the parent.*

— FRANK PITTMAN

YOU'VE SPENT SO LONG PREPARING for this moment, and now that
it's here, you're not quite sure what happens next. Those first few
moments might go by in a blur of emotions and tears and a flurry
of activity from the doctors and nurses. Before you know it,
someone has handed you a baby and congratulated you on
becoming a father. This is it: the culmination of all those sleepless
nights anticipating their arrival and pointless arguments over
trivial things like the shade of the wallpaper in the nursery. All of
that seems so unnecessary now that you're staring into the face of
your child. They're probably a lot smaller than you thought they'd
be, and they look so fragile and vulnerable. So, what comes next?
It's okay to feel uncertain. Knowing you're about to become a

father isn't the same as having physical evidence of your fatherhood placed in your arms.

Every little stretch and squeak they make paralyzes you with anxiety because you're not sure what they need or if you're holding them the correct way. None of the parenting books prepared you for this. In fact, you probably can't recall a single helpful thing you've learned about holding a newborn or interpreting crying cues. In this chapter, we'll be tentatively taking those first few awkward steps into fatherhood. From the initial awe of meeting your child to the terrifying realization that it's now your responsibility to care for this new life, we'll be facing that daunting prospect together and figuring out how best to navigate these unchartered waters.

Essential Guidance for the Immediate Postpartum Period

The miracle of childbirth is a joy to behold and a unique experience that you'll likely never forget. But it's also draining, emotional, and highly taxing on your partner. They're probably going to want to rest after giving birth, no matter if they delivered vaginally or had a caesarean. One important consideration for that first hour immediately after giving birth is for your partner to bond with the baby.

The doctor might place the baby on your partner's chest and encourage her to attempt breastfeeding if that's the route she's chosen to take. You might feel out of place, not knowing how to be supportive or get involved, but there's no reason you can't be a part of that process. If there's a lactation specialist around or a nurse offering your partner breastfeeding advice, listen in. Maybe write down some key points and helpful tips they might provide. Your partner is probably so exhausted that they'll forget half of what is being said.

While your partner is breastfeeding or having skin-to-skin bonding with the baby, you can place a hand on their back or hold their little hand. You're a family now, so find a way to feel included. Ask your partner if there's anything they need or anything you can get for them.

Skin-To-Skin Contact

Skin-to-skin contact (also known as kangaroo care) is when you place your naked baby on your bare chest. It's an essential way for newborns to bond with their parents. Yes, parents, that means you can do it too! Usually, doctors will encourage your partner to have skin-to-skin contact with the baby for the first hour after they're born. This first hour is a crucial time for bonding with the baby and allowing them to acclimate to the outside world. If your partner is unable to do it for any reason, you can take over. Having the comfort of that closeness is very healthy for your baby's development and will help them form healthy bonds with you and your partner.

Having felt like an outsider for the duration of the pregnancy, having skin-to-skin contact with your baby in those first few hours will help you begin to create that essential bond with your child. It will also give you an opportunity to get to experience the marvel of their existence in a way you've probably been dying to for months.

Not only is skin-to-skin contact an incredible way to bond with your baby, but it also helps regulate their temperature and heart rate and stabilizes their blood pressure and blood glucose levels. Babies who are given skin-to-skin contact also cry less and sleep better.

Physical Recovery After Birth

Pregnancy might be over, but your partner still has quite a long way to go before their body is back to normal. In particular, the first six weeks postpartum might be the most challenging. No matter how your partner gave birth, their body is going to be a little worse for wear. Their muscles are probably sore from labor and the stress that the whole process puts their body through. If they gave birth vaginally, they're likely experiencing a lot of pain and discomfort as their vagina heals from that. Those who've had a caesarean are nursing that wound too. All of this can make it very difficult for your partner to be up and about in those early weeks. And that's not even mentioning the baby.

A newborn needs to be fed every two hours, so for those first few days, it can seem like that's all your partner does. They may find themselves glued to the couch for days on end, which can become frustrating for both of you.

Emotionally, your partner's hormones are still all over the place. Her body is trying to recover from the pregnancy, but it will take a while for her hormone levels to stabilize properly. This can add stress to an already intense transitional period.

Supporting Your Partner's Physical Postpartum Healing

Now that the baby is finally here, you can get a lot more involved as a parent, especially during the postpartum period, when your partner probably needs some time to rest and heal. If you're looking for the best ways to support your partner during this time, I'm here to help!

You've probably heard of *baby brain* and assumed it was some sort of urban legend, but it's real! With everything going on, it's no surprise that your partner might seem a bit out of sorts a lot of the time. You can support her through this by making sure that all the important things get done. Set reminders for appointments you might have and stay on top of her schedule. Hopefully, she shouldn't have too many commitments for the time being, but the little things are easily forgotten. She's probably so focused on taking care of the baby that she completely forgets to take care of herself.

Make sure she's eating regular meals and remembering to stay hydrated. Whether or not she's breastfeeding, she'll need to take in a lot of nutrients. Pregnancy depletes a mother's own store of vital nutrients, so it's essential that she replace them with healthy, regular meals. If she is breastfeeding, she'll need them even more.

Create a few little hydration and snack stations around the house to make it easier for her to remember to nourish and take care of herself. Place these stations in areas where she might normally sit and feed the baby. It's also a good idea to maybe put things like magazines, phone chargers, and other little essential items she might need in these areas too. Once the baby falls asleep, it's likely that she's not going to want to move. It will be very helpful for her to have the things she might need nearby.

With the baby mostly feeding and sleeping in those early days, you'd be forgiven if you still felt a little left out, but you don't have to. Get involved by learning how to sterilize bottles, store pumped breastmilk, or prepare formula bottles if you can. Offer to change a few diapers or help put the baby to sleep. Take advantage of any opportunity you can find to bond with your baby; I'm sure your partner will also appreciate the break. If possible, wake up a little earlier and take over looking after the baby so your partner can get a few hours of extra sleep.

Make a point of regularly asking your partner if there's anything she needs or if there's anything you can do or get for her. Again, she'll be so wrapped up in caring for the baby that she'll often neglect her own needs. While she's wrapped up in looking after the baby, you should make sure to look after her!

Here are some ways you can help your partner cope with physical discomfort postpartum:

- If your partner is experiencing extreme muscular discomfort, encourage her to stay off her feet. Offer her regular massages and maybe even some OTC medication. If she's breastfeeding, make sure you talk to her doctor about this first.
- A postpartum belly band is a useful tool that will help relieve some of the pain your partner is experiencing in her back and stomach. A belly band also offers comfort for those who've had a C-section.
- Dry and cracked nipples can make breastfeeding unbearable. Run out and get your partner some lanolin and nipple creams. Many of them are made with ingredients that are baby-safe so she doesn't have to worry about wiping them off before feeding.
- Ice packs are great for a myriad of reasons. They can both soothe muscle pain and also bring relief to vaginal and perineal pain and discomfort following natural birth.

Be proactive in lending a helping hand around the house wherever needed, especially in those early days while your partner is healing and still adjusting to this new responsibility. Housework and laundry should be the last thing she has to worry about. You should also do your best to be as involved with the baby as you can. This isn't to say that you should become Superman and do everything; delegate! If you have close friends and family who are willing and able to help lessen the load, reach out to them for help with things like bringing prepared meals or helping with a little tidying around the house. Your partner isn't the only one who deserves a bit of rest!

Postpartum Emotional Adjustment

The postpartum period is about more than just physically healing from giving birth; it's also about emotionally adjusting to your new roles as parents and coping with everything that it entails. It's normal to feel like you're both in a bit of an emotional freefall in those early days. So much is happening, and you barely have time to think about how you're feeling because you're so stressed about the baby. Panicking about not knowing why they're crying or if they've eaten enough—terrified that you're changing their diapers wrong or they're not getting enough sleep.

There's a bit of a sweet spot immediately after giving birth. You're still glowing from the realization of your new role and the awe of meeting your child for the first time. There are still all the nurses and doctors around, and it makes you feel safe with the baby, knowing that if anything goes wrong, someone nearby can fix it. And then they hand you the baby and send you home; that's when reality really sets in. That's when you need to pray that everything you learned in those prenatal classes is enough to help you care for your newborn.

The Baby Blues

Many women suffer from what is called the baby blues or postpartum blues. It normally starts within a day or two of giving birth and lasts a few days or weeks. When you think of everything your partner has just endured and is now faced with, it's not surprising she might be feeling a little overwhelmed.

The baby blues can bring about feelings of sadness in your partner and cause symptoms such as:

- crying spells
- trouble sleeping
- loss of appetite
- irritability
- trouble concentrating

Your partner might feel overwhelmed by the responsibilities involved in looking after the baby at times, appear moody, and struggle to make decisions. The baby blues can be caused by a variety of factors. Your partner might still be reeling from the experience of giving birth and how much that took out of her, both physically and emotionally. There's also the fact that her hormones are still readjusting after the pregnancy and need some time to get back to normal. That, coupled with the sleepless nights and all the stress and anxiety associated with becoming a new parent, is enough to get anyone feeling a little down. The good news about the baby blues is that they normally go away on their own and don't require medical intervention.

Postpartum Depression

In some cases, the sadness doesn't go away on its own after two weeks. Some women continue to struggle with feelings of sadness that are so intense that they infringe on their ability to care for their new baby. If you feel that your partner falls into this category, then they might be suffering from a medical condition known as postpartum depression.

Postpartum depression affects many mothers without them even being aware of it. Some might even feel too afraid or ashamed to openly express how they're feeling because they think people will judge them. We as a society are so used to thinking of babies as being an inherently good thing that we find it impossible to imagine how anyone could not find parenthood to be an utterly captivating experience. This expectation makes it difficult for mothers to speak up when they're having feelings of sadness or anxiety about their new role as parents.

Some symptoms of postpartum depression include:

- feeling detached from the baby.
- withdrawing from the baby, you, and other close friends and family
- feeling hopeless and helpless.
- trouble sleeping, even when the baby is asleep.
- crying often and without cause.
- suicidal thoughts.
- feeling overwhelmed constantly.
- worrying that they or someone else might harm the baby.

Should your partner express any of these thoughts or feelings with you, it's important that you notice that they might be suffering from postpartum depression and get them the help that they need. Unlike the baby blues, postpartum depression doesn't go away on its own and will likely only worsen the longer it goes untreated.

Be supportive of your partner, and let them know that they are not a bad parent or a bad person for having these thoughts and feelings. Postpartum depression is an illness, and it's not their fault. Validate their feelings, and don't try to disprove or dismiss them.

Some ways you can help your partner through postpartum depression are:

- make sure they're getting sleep. Offer to take over caring for the baby for a few hours so they can get some rest.
- make sure they're taking time for themselves. New mothers often neglect themselves, so encouraging your partner to do things like eat, shower, read a book, or watch an episode of their favorite show, is a good way to help them destress and unwind.
- take initiative in doing things for them to make their lives a little easier. Sometimes it isn't helpful to ask them what they need because they probably don't know. Be proactive and do things that you know will help them, without them having to ask.

The most beneficial thing you can do for your partner, however, is to get them the help that they need. Talk to a medical professional about what their options are, and get them into a treatment program as soon as possible.

Believe it or not, postpartum depression doesn't just affect mothers; you, too, might be at risk. New fathers can also be prone to postpartum depression. Unfortunately, it's often overlooked or missed because, unlike your partner, you're not kept under the watchful eye of medical professionals after the birth.

Depression in new fathers can be the result of:

- expectations
- struggling to adjust to your new role as a father
- lack of external support
- sleep deprivation
- changes in your relationship

It's important that you be able to spot the potential risk factors and signs of postpartum depression in yourself, because, even if your partner has it, it won't manifest the same way in both of you.

If you often find yourself feeling insecure about your competence as a father or getting angry and irritable for no reason, you might be suffering from postpartum depression. Although the chances of you having it are higher if your partner has it, you can also get it even if your partner doesn't.

Societal pressures for men to be the head of the household and adopt a stoic persona have made it difficult for men to reach out for help when they're struggling. But I promise you, asking for help doesn't make you any less of a man. To be honest, I ended up going for a bit of therapy myself after becoming a father. I had been feeling anxious for quite some time towards the end of the pregnancy, wrestling with thoughts of inadequacy surrounding my new role as a father. I knew the kind of father I wanted to be, but I wasn't sure if I had the capability to live up to it. My own father was a traditional family man; he provided a roof over my head and food in my stomach but not much emotional support. I wanted to be different, but without an example to follow, I was scared that I was going to fail and end up just like him. Going to therapy to discuss and explore these fears and anxieties really helped alleviate a lot of that tension for me. Having a safe space to just lay it all out on the table and be honest instead of putting on a brave face and acting like I knew what I was doing was so refreshing.

Sure, I was reluctant at first because I wasn't exactly raised to believe in those things, but I've never regretted going. Not only did it help me communicate better with my partner, but it gave me perspective on so many of the thoughts that were bogging me down. I realized that fatherhood was a journey and that I could learn on the job. I didn't need to have it all figured out from the get-go. I was stressed about how I was going to teach my son how to be a good man when all I needed to know at that point was how to change a diaper.

As much as this journey has been about supporting your partner, it's also about knowing when you might need a little support yourself. This isn't an easy road to walk, so don't try to tough it out and go it alone. Be there for your partner, especially in those early days. She's endured a lot throughout pregnancy and childbirth and could probably use more than a little TLC. Soothe her aches and pains and encourage her to put her feet up for a while. Remember that stepping up doesn't mean shouldering all of the responsibilities yourself. Use your network of support to get things done; don't be afraid to delegate.

Finding your feet in those early days can be hard and can bring up a lot of emotions for both your partner and yourself. Familiarize yourself with the signs of postpartum depression so you can be prepared should your partner start to exhibit any of them. Look out for them in yourself as well. Becoming a parent is already hard, so make sure you're looking after yourselves and each other if you want to give yourselves the best shot at being the best parents you can be.

NEWBORN AND INFANT CARE

7

———

FIRST DAYS AND WEEKS–A COMPREHENSIVE GUIDE

Life doesn't get more real than having a newborn at home.

— ERIC CHURCH

AFTER THE ROLLERCOASTER of pregnancy and childbirth, you'd be forgiven for riding on a pink cloud for a little while. You're in absolute awe of your child, and you can't stop marveling at how perfect they are. Probably while they are sleeping, you find yourself captivated by the delight of manipulating their adorable fingers and toes. Nothing brings you crashing down to reality as fast as a crying baby, though. When you're holding a screaming newborn and trying to guess what's wrong, suddenly, the enchantment of being a parent isn't quite so blissful. Panic sets in, and you're sweating a little. You don't want to wake your partner to ask for help because she really needs these few extra hours of sleep and you want to prove to her (and yourself) that you're perfectly capable of looking after the baby on your own. But, are you really? How does your partner already know what the baby's various cries signify? They all sound the same to you! Calm down;

I've got you. In this chapter, we'll be getting down to the nitty-gritty part of your new role as a father. From changing diapers to burping and solving the riddle of endless crying, this is probably the chapter you'll want to keep bookmarked on your phone for when things start getting a little too real in the newborn department!

Practical Advice on Newborn Care

Don't be fooled by that cute little face; taking care of a newborn is a lot of work! Not only do they require constant attention, but they're unable to vocalize their needs, which means you're left playing guessing games about what they might need. Here's some advice: It's normal sleep, food, burp, or nappy. So, let's tackle those four needs first and see how you can best attend to them.

Feeding the Baby

If your partner has chosen to breastfeed, you might feel excluded, but this doesn't have to be the case. Even though you can't actively participate, that doesn't mean you can't offer support. Breastfeeding isn't something that comes naturally to most mothers, despite what you may think. You may find that your partner struggles to get the baby to latch correctly and, as a result, breastfeeding causes her a lot of pain and discomfort.

Finding a lactation consultant who can come and give your partner tips and advice on how to get your baby to latch and the correct way to hold the baby during feedings can be a great help. If you struggle to find one, there are plenty of online resources you can turn to that will guide you through the process. Look up different things your partner can try to make breastfeeding easier. Spend some time researching while she's busy with the baby and find strategies and techniques that might be helpful to her.

Supporting your partner while she's breastfeeding is also a great way to feel more involved. Offer her some pillows to help get her into a more comfortable position because those breastfeeding sessions can be really long! You should also encourage her to stay hydrated and get her a jug of water to work her way through. Milk production can really leave her feeling dehydrated.

If she's struggling with her milk supply, there are various ways you can help stimulate her milk production. Making her teas that contain fenugreek and flaxseed is recommended, or you can buy her some nursing tea from a local health store. If you're feeling adventurous, you can strap on an apron and bake her some lactation cookies! These tasty treats are easy to make, and you can easily find a recipe for them online.

Should you wish to get more hands-on, ask your partner to pump some milk that you can then use to bottle feed the baby. This will be especially useful if you'd like to help with the night feedings so your partner can get some rest. Remember to properly wash and sterilize your bottles and check the temperature of the milk before you feed the baby.

If your partner has chosen not to breastfeed, you can share the responsibility of feeding the baby, taking turns throughout the day, and then taking shifts for overnight feedings. Remember to follow the proper directions for preparing the formula; don't try to eyeball it; this isn't a cocktail!

Bottle-feeding is a great way for you to bond with the baby, so try to be fully present during the process. Merely placing a bottle against their head and hoping for the best is insufficient. Hold them, make eye contact, and talk to them. It might seem like a lot, but they're only this small for such a short amount of time. These are the little moments you'll look back on and treasure. Even if they usually culminate with you covered in spit-up.

Sterilizing Bottles

Whether you're formula feeding or your partner is expressing milk, you must keep the baby's bottles as sterile as possible. Your newborn's immune system is still getting stronger, so the best thing you can do for them is expose them to as few germs and bacteria as possible.

The traditional way of sterilizing these items is to boil them. Make sure you disassemble them first and give them a good wash with soap and warm water. Next, place them in a pot and fill the pot with water until it covers the items completely. Then, put the pot on the stove and bring the water to a boil for five minutes. Remove the items with tongs and place them on a clean towel, ready for use when you need them.

It's a good idea to sterilize these items at least once a day while your baby is under two months old. Remember to sterilize any new items you buy before using them.

Burping the Baby

Speaking of spit-up, one of the most important parts of feeding your baby is remembering to burp them. Now, this can seem terrifying at first because newborns look so fragile, so I'm going to guide you through it.

The reason you need to burp your baby during and after feeding is that they swallow air bubbles while they drink, whether they're breastfed or bottle-fed. These trapped air bubbles can make them feel uncomfortable, and you might notice them starting to get cranky and squirm around. The only way to release these air bubbles is to pat them out.

The best positions to use when burping a baby are:

- Hold your baby on your chest with their head on your shoulder while sitting in an upright position. Support them with one hand and use the other to pat them on the back.
- Sit your baby up on your knee, using one hand to hold their head and support their neck. You can rub or pat them on the back, and you can even try bouncing them a little to help the air bubble come up.
- Lay your baby face down on your lap, remembering to support their head with one hand. Angle your legs so that their head is higher than their chest. Pat them on the back with your other hand.

When burping a baby, it's gentler for them to use a cupped hand rather than a flat palm. You should also drape a spit cloth over your shoulder or across your lap to catch any possible spit-up in case they have a wet burp.

Changing the Baby's Diaper

You're probably not a fan of diaper changes, but don't worry, nobody is. It's just one of those things that needs to get done. The good news is that the process gets easier the more you practice. Eventually, you'll be able to do it in your sleep. Literally, because you'll probably be doing it many times in the middle of the night.

Your first few attempts at changing a diaper are going to be unpleasant. Firstly, because you're confused and unsure of what you're doing. Secondly, because you might gag, seriously, it's not for the faint of heart. But you'll get through it and, eventually, get used to it.

Here's a step-by-step guide to changing a diaper:

1. Be prepared

It'll go a lot quicker if you have everything you need at arm's length before you start. This will also prevent you from having to turn your back on the baby to get something because they might roll off the changing table and injure themselves. This can happen in the blink of an eye, so to avoid catastrophe, never take your eyes off the baby. It's also probably a good idea to keep one hand on the baby throughout the changing process for the same reason.

Before you even bring the baby to the changing table, make sure you have a fresh diaper, wet wipes, bum cream, and a plastic bag ready to take the dirty diaper.

2. Clean your hands

Make sure to wash and sanitize your hands to keep germs from passing on to the baby. You should also probably remove any rings or jewelry you're wearing that could scratch their sensitive skin. If your hands are cold, give them a good rub to get the blood going. Cold hands can make for a cranky baby!

3. Lift your baby onto the changing table

If you don't have a changing table, any flat, stable surface will do. Cover the surface with a blanket or cloth to make your baby comfortable and to avoid making a mess.

4. Open the diaper

Unfold the flaps on the side of the diaper and fold them back so they don't stick to your baby's skin.

5. Fold down the top part of the diaper

Once the diaper is open, you can see what you're working with. If there's poop, you can use the folded top part to scoop some of it off, as it's likely there's still some poop stuck on the baby's skin.

You should also use a wet wipe to clean the rest of the poop off the baby. Avoid using scented wipes or wipes containing alcohol, as this can irritate your baby's skin. The more natural, the better. Lift the infant's legs in order to reach underneath them, and be sure to clean the creases on their thighs as well. Poop has a habit of sneaking in there.

6. **The switch over**

Remove the soiled diaper from underneath the baby and replace it with a fresh one. Try to get this part done as quickly as possible. Babies have the nasty habit of choosing that exact moment to urinate. Some parents place the new diaper under the baby even before removing the soiled one, but I've never been able to unlock that skill level yet.

Remember to place the dirty diaper away from your child's reach. You don't even want to know what can happen if they get their hands on it. It's not pretty.

7. **Apply the bum cream**

Ensure that the diaper area of your infant is completely dry prior to applying the diaper cream. Leaving them damp from wet wipes can cause a rash.

8. **Close the diaper**

When you're closing the diaper, make sure you don't strap it too tight. Ideally, you should still be able to squeeze two fingers in between the nappy and the skin from the top. Make sure the diaper aligns with the belly button, and don't forget to release the waterproof flaps on the side.

9. Clean your hands

Make sure you thoroughly sanitize your hands before you pick your baby up again, also because you might have accidentally gotten some poop on your hands in the process. Don't worry, it happens.

And that's it! Congratulations on a successful diaper change! Now, just get ready to repeat this another half a dozen or so times throughout the day and night, and you'll be a pro in no time!

The Science of Sleep

Newborns do a lot of sleeping, so it's important that you know both how to help them get to sleep and how to ensure that they're sleeping safely.

Safe Sleep

Ensuring that your baby is sleeping safely is as easy as ABC—literally! Let's look at the ABCs of safe sleep:

A: Alone

A baby is safest if they're sleeping alone. A lot of new parents, often overexerted and sleep-deprived, fall asleep with their newborns either lying on the couch or sitting watching TV. Some mothers might fall asleep with their baby beside them on the bed after breastfeeding. Unfortunately, these scenarios aren't safe for the baby, as they increase the likelihood of something bad happening. Without realizing it, you might roll over onto your infant, or a blanket or piece of bedding could suffocate them.

The safest way for your baby to sleep is alone, unencumbered by things like toys, blankets, or cot bumpers. Sure, having a bunch of stuffies in their cot is cute for Instagram posts, but having a cluttered sleeping space poses a hazard for your baby.

B: Back

As much as we're all enamored by those cute images of babies sleeping on their stomachs with their bums in the air, the safest way for your baby to sleep is on their back. This is the best way to make sure their airways are clear, and nothing is obstructing their face. Whenever you put your newborn down to sleep, make sure you always put them down on their backs.

C: Crib

Babies should always be put to sleep in a crib. The crib should have nothing but a fitted sheet and a firm mattress to prevent them from getting stuck in something or having something obstruct their airways. If your baby falls asleep in their car seat during a trip, don't leave them there. Transfer them to their crib as soon as you get home.

Don't sleep with your baby in your bed with you, or allow them to sleep with a sibling, as this isn't safe for them. They can sleep in your room, provided they're in their crib or bassinet.

Sudden Infant Death Syndrome

SIDS (Sudden Infant Death Syndrome) is the unexplained death of an infant under the age of one year and is a fear for many new parents. Although we still don't know what the exact cause of SIDS is, following safe sleeping practices has been proven to drastically decrease the risk of your baby succumbing to it. Some other ways to decrease your baby's risk of SIDS are:

- avoid smoking around your baby
- encourage your partner to breastfeed

- keep up to date with your baby's immunizations
- don't overdress your baby for sleep; this will prevent them from overheating
- put the baby to sleep with a pacifier

Co-Sleeping

Ultimately, your baby's sleeping arrangements are up to you. Some parents find that co-sleeping works best for them. When we refer to co-sleeping, people may have differing definitions of what that means. For some, co-sleeping refers to bed-sharing with the baby. For others, co-sleeping simply refers to having the baby's crib or bassinet in the parent's bedroom.

Having a crib in your room can be beneficial for many reasons. Firstly, it makes night feedings a lot easier if the baby is nearby. It's also much quicker to get to the baby if they start crying. It gives parents comfort knowing that their baby is close by as well, should anything happen to them.

Despite it being against medical advice, many parents still choose to share a bed with their infants for personal reasons. A lot of new parents crave that closeness with their newborn and feel that it's easier to breastfeed throughout the night if the baby is nearby. It's still important to note that bed-sharing significantly increases the risk of infant injury, even more so if:

- your baby is pre-term
- your baby is bed-sharing with a parent who is under the influence of a substance or extremely fatigued
- your infant is bed-sharing with someone other than a primary caregiver
- one of the parents is a smoker

- your bed has a soft mattress, pillows, blankets, or anything else that might expose them to suffocation or overheating

Should you and your partner choose to co-sleep with your baby, try and make it as safe as possible. Place them on their back, remove any possible dangers from the area, and make sure they don't overheat.

Learning Your Baby's Cues

I used to think my partner had a telepathic connection with the baby. She always seemed to know what the baby needed or why they were crying. It was almost as if she knew instinctively or was deciphering an unknown message in the tone and pitch of the baby's cries. It wasn't until much later that I realized that she was simply interpreting the baby's cues.

Although newborns can't speak, they're still able to communicate their needs with their parents. They do this by using various cues that you can look out for. There are specific cues related to their different needs, such as food, sleep, or comfort. By learning the signs to look out for, you, too, can fool people into believing that you're telepathic.

Being able to respond to your baby's cues is important because it facilitates their development. It will also help your baby feel safe and secure knowing that their needs are being met, and it will help you grow and strengthen your connection to your baby.

Tired

Here are some signs to look out for that tell you that your baby is tired and might need a nap:

- unfocused gaze or staring off into space
- yawning
- stretching
- waving their arms and legs
- losing interest in whatever they were doing
- making jerky movements
- pulling at their ears
- rubbing their eyes

Hungry

Here are some signs to look out for that tell you that your baby is hungry and probably needs to be fed:

- opening and closing their mouth
- sucking on their fingers or putting their fist in their mouth
- looking around for a nipple with their mouth
- sticking their tongue out
- licking their lips

Playtime

Here are some signs to look out for that tell you that your baby wants to interact and play with you:

- they're awake and alert
- their eyes follow you intently
- they grab onto objects or your finger
- they bring their hands and feet together
- they reach their hands out to you
- they smile at you

Time-out

Here are some signs to look out for that tell you that your baby has grown bored of the activity or needs a bit of a break:

- turning their head away from you
- they frown or begin to fuss and cry
- they become tense
- they stretch out their arms and spread out their fingers
- they begin to squirm and arch their back

These cues are just a basic guideline for what you can look out for. Of course, each baby is different, and they might not display these exact cues or use them in different ways. The great thing about learning to interpret your baby's cues is that you can quickly meet their needs and attend to their discomfort before it escalates to crying. The more time you spend with your baby, the better you'll get at being able to understand what their cues mean.

Look at you, parenting like a pro! When you think of newborn care as a whole, it can seem daunting and intimidating, but when you break it down into its individual facets and break those things down into easy steps, you realize it's really not that bad. Sure, the frequency of the tasks can be a bit overwhelming at first, but as time passes, you'll get better at them, and they'll require less frequent attention. The more time you spend getting to know your baby and learning how to take care of them, the more comfortable and confident you'll become in your ability to look after them. Stepping into the unknown is scary for anyone, and fatherhood is a pretty big unknown. But with time and patience, your anxiety will diminish. Being actively involved in taking care of your newborn will not only fill you with a sense of purpose and help you feel more like a parent, but the bond you'll grow with your baby will give you a joy you've never experienced before.

Getting to see them go from a helpless newborn who couldn't hold their own head up to a cute little baby with a budding personality is a remarkable journey. In the next chapter, we'll be exploring the various milestones you can celebrate along the way and when you can expect your baby to start slowly gaining independence.

8

CELEBRATING GROWTH—
MILESTONES IN THE FIRST YEAR

There's nobody as brave as a baby taking his/her first non-stop 5 steps alone from Mummy's hand to daddy's hand... trust me on that.

— SAMEH ELSAYED

WE'VE all seen that dramatic moment when a baby takes their first steps enacted in films countless times. I used to roll my eyes every time the scene unfolded, refusing to believe that something as trivial as a child taking a single step before falling straight back down could illicit such a deep emotional reaction from a grown adult. Of course, now I know better. What truly shocked me wasn't that I became emotional the first time my baby took a few unassisted steps; it was that I became emotional at nearly every milestone. I hadn't thought of that before; I had never pictured the journey from newborn to toddler or beyond, and it's truly remarkable.

To see a baby who couldn't do a single thing for themselves suddenly sitting up by themselves or lifting a spoon from their mouth is truly a feeling that nothing can prepare you for. In this chapter, we'll be breaking down the first year into milestones and developmental markers for which you can keep an eye out. Milestones aren't just about celebrating; they're also a way for you to keep track of your child's development so you can have an early warning if anything goes amiss. Keep in mind, however, that every child is different and develops in their own way and at their own pace. This is just a guideline; if you're concerned about your child's development, you should speak to their doctor.

The First Three Months

At first, it might seem like your newborn does little other than feed, cry, and sleep, but even in those early days, you can start to see some growth and development.

First Month

In the first month, your baby will begin to develop their reflexes; you'll be able to see them reacting to bright lights or flinching at loud sounds. They might even turn towards the sound of a familiar voice and, if you're lucky, even smile!

They'll need to start strengthening their neck muscles, and you can help them by placing them on their stomachs on a playmat for brief periods at a time. This is called tummy time, and it's the best way to help them learn how to use their muscles. In that first month, they might be able to lift their head for brief periods and move their head from side to side.

Second Month

By the second month, their communication has evolved from only crying to making gurgling and cooing sounds. They may smile when they hear your voice or smile back at you if you smile at them. Their eyesight is getting better, and they might try to follow moving objects with their eyes. You can help them improve this by holding a toy above their head and moving it around slowly, allowing them to track it with their eyes.

During tummy time, they should now be able to push themselves up with their arms into something that looks like a yoga pose. They should also have much better control of their head and neck movements, although they'll still need to be supported when you hold them.

Third Month

By the third month, your baby is getting more animated, making funny faces, and trying to imitate your facial expressions. They should be able to recognize the sound of your voice by now and turn toward you when they hear you entering a room.

If you've been diligent with your tummy time, they might also be able to lift themselves up onto their arms, sort of like a seal. You'll notice that they've started imitating sounds, so be sure to talk to them as often as you can to help boost their language and communication development.

Talk to them as if having a normal conversation, and narrate everything you do. This will help them learn the words of things and the meanings of actions. You might feel silly having full-blown conversations with someone who does nothing but blow raspberries at you in response, but I promise, it will pay off!

Three to Six Months

Fourth Month

Prepare your heart to hear your baby's first giggle because it might just explode. I'd never heard a more amazing sound than my child's first laugh, and I suddenly began making an absolute fool of myself in an attempt to elicit another one. Your baby has started to recognize your face and voice and will turn to follow you around the room or make sounds to try and get your attention.

Their head and neck muscles have developed enough that they can hold their own heads up now, and they've become a lot less stationary. Be prepared for the rolling! Your baby might learn to roll from their tummy onto their back, so don't leave them unattended on a changing table, not even for a second!

You may find that they can recognize objects now and have a favorite toy. Make sure you never leave the house without it. They're also learning how to grab things, so keep any dangling jewelry out of their reach. Trust me, there's nothing stronger than a baby's grip. You'll need the jaws of life to pry those tiny fingers open.

Your baby has also started developing their leg muscles now and will kick their feet while holding their body up during tummy time. You can also feel them pushing down with their legs when you hold them up.

Fifth Month

Your baby can now probably roll from their tummy to their back and vice versa, so keep your eyes open! You wouldn't think that someone could get very far just by rolling, but you're in for a shock. You might leave your baby in one corner of the room, and within seconds, it's like they're all the way on the other side, grasping at your charging cable and trying to put it into their mouth.

Using their mouths to explore things is a normal part of their development, so make sure you keep anything potentially hazardous far away from those pincers. Their motor development will probably improve, and you can observe them switching objects from one hand to the other.

Those curious eyes are also still taking everything in, and you might notice them starting to take an interest in what you're eating. This is a signal that they might be ready to start being introduced to solid foods, but make sure to first check with your doctor.

Your baby is becoming a lot more playful now and enjoys playing with toys and interactive games like peekaboo. They could probably play peekaboo for hours without getting bored, and you'll notice them getting upset when playtime is over.

Sixth Month

This month, your baby might start recognizing their own name. They're also learning to recognize themselves and will love spending time looking at their own reflection in the mirror.

Your conversations are no longer one-sided, as your baby may start babbling back at you when you talk to them. They'll start making more vowel and consonant sounds as they start learning how to use language to communicate. For now, they're just getting the hang of the basics.

Speaking of the basics, your baby might start sitting up this month! Where has the time gone? You might also catch them rocking back and forth on their hands and knees, a warning that they might be crawling soon.

You can put their grabby hands to good use by letting them feed themselves finger foods or trying out the use of a spoon. Be careful, because it's probably going to get very messy. Be prepared to scrub pea puree off the windows and possibly out of your hair.

Six to Nine Months

Has it really been half a year already? With everything going on, it's easy to lose track of time. As we get older, we stop to really take notice of the passage of time. It's not until you have a baby in the house that you realize just how much can change in a short span of time. It is hard to believe that only a few months ago, your infant was primarily able to eat and sleep. However, that time has flown by, and they are now actively developing their own distinct personality!

Seventh Month

Your baby is starting to both recognize and display emotions. They respond to your facial expressions, whether happy or stern, and express their own joy through laughter. They will also whine or cry when they're upset, especially when you tell them playtime is over. *No* has become their least favorite word, and they understand what it means now, even if they pretend that they don't.

Their babbling is becoming more coherent, and they'll probably repeat the same sounds over and over, so don't get too excited if you think you hear them saying mama or dada; they're not quite there yet.

They will likely be able to sit up on their own without any help and be able to support their weight on their feet if you hold them under their armpits. Their hands are also becoming more adept, and they have started to pull objects towards themselves using a raking motion. Again, be careful of those grabby hands!

Eighth Month

During the eighth month, your baby might start pulling themselves up on objects and into a standing position, so make sure anything unstable they might use is out of the way. They might not crawl yet but could start scooting themselves around on their bum, so keep a watchful eye.

Stranger danger has set in, and you might suddenly find yourself with a very clingy baby. Separation anxiety around this age is normal, but don't worry; it will pass. In the meantime, get used to having them glued to either you or your partner for the foreseeable future.

Expect a lot of drooling to occur as many babies start cutting their first teeth. Keep a spit cloth or bib nearby at all times because it's probably going to get pretty messy. Getting a couple of teething toys will probably help, as well as some teething gel from the drugstore to relieve the aches and pains.

Ninth Month

Your baby is officially on the move! A lot of babies begin to crawl at this age, which can be both exciting and terrifying because they move at lightning speed!

Now that they're mobile, their curiosity moves into hyperdrive, and no object is safe from their explorations. If you haven't thoroughly baby-proofed your house, now is definitely the time to do so to prevent accidents and heartbreak. I know I learned the hard way when I mistakenly left a cord hanging a little too low and lost my PlayStation as a result when it came crashing down to its death.

A good way to keep your baby from causing chaos is to put them in a playpen and surround them with toys to keep them busy so you can do things around the house without having a mild panic attack every time you hear a loud noise.

Your baby enjoys playing interactive games with you and now understands to look for objects when you hide them behind something. They're also a lot more expressive and may start to communicate with you by pointing at things that they want or lifting their arms when they want you to pick them up.

Nine to Twelve Months

It's probably hard to believe that your baby has now been out of the womb for the same amount of time as they were in the womb and has probably developed just as fast! You've probably more or less settled into fatherhood now and are less anxious about breaking them as they've gotten bigger and more durable. As much chaos as they may cause, you can't imagine your home without their lively laughter or ear-piercing cries.

Tenth Month

Cover your ears because things just got loud! Your baby has started experimenting with their toys and other objects by banging them together to see what sound they make. The louder, the better! Save yourself by buying them a rattle to shake or a little drum to bang away on.

They've also mastered the skill of lifting themselves up using furniture and can cruise around by holding onto things for support. You can help them by placing stable furniture along their path that they can use to meander their way around.

Their communication continues to improve, as they're now able to shake their heads *no* when they don't want something and might even give you a wave of hello or goodbye. They're able to respond to the sound of their name and can recognize the names of familiar objects.

Eleventh Month

Keep your camera nearby because you might be able to catch some incredible moments this month. Your baby may say their first words or take their first steps on their own.

They're beginning to understand a lot more of the world around them and might mimic things you do, such as pushing buttons, opening drawers, or pretending to talk on the phone.

They can also point to objects when you name them and understand basic commands, such as *stop that* or *don't touch*. Not that they're likely going to obey them. You might finally get to hear them call you dada for the first time, a moment that will stay with you for the rest of your life. Although, within a few months, you'll probably get tired of hearing it.

Twelfth Month

From the moment your baby begins to walk, they are no longer considered a baby. They are now toddlers. It's a scary realization, but time really does go by so quickly.

By now, your baby is such a far cry from the helpless newborn you once held anxiously as you tried to figure out why they were crying. They can name things, express their emotions, and use gestures to indicate what they want.

They're able to walk, although they might still prefer crawling as they get their bearings. Their explorations have resulted in them being able to use objects correctly. Like using a spoon to eat or a brush to comb their hair. They're probably still quite the messy eater, but they're trying! They can also use a sippy cup now and maybe a regular cup with a little help.

They enjoy playing and spending time with you and might cry when you leave the room. They're a lot more interactive now, and they like playing peekaboo or pat-a-cake. They understand that you should look for objects when you hide them.

They're still playing garage band with everything in sight, banging, dropping, and hitting things together to see what sounds they make. They have started to show a preference for things like toys and people.

Although they might still be babies, they've come a long way. However, they still have a long way to go!

Pat yourself on the back; you've successfully survived the first year of parenting!

9

NAVIGATING CHALLENGES WITH CONFIDENCE

Being a father means you have to think fast on your feet. You must be judicious, wise, brave, tender, and willing to put on a frilly hat and sit down to a pretend tea party.

— MATTHEW BUCKLEY

AS MUCH AS we all wish for an easy transition into fatherhood, the reality is that life still happens. The best thing you can do is hope for the best but prepare for the worst. Understand that this new role you're taking on isn't going to be without difficulties. No matter how much planning we think we did during pregnancy, sometimes unexpected things happen. Learn to roll with the punches and take it in stride. In this chapter, we're going to be looking at some of the obstacles you might come across and how best to navigate your way through them. Remember that taking care of a newborn isn't easy for anyone, even couples who've had children before. And then there are your other obligations, such as finding a balance between your new responsibilities as a father and still being able to meet the demands of your professional career. In all this, you might just lose yourself, as new fathers often do. Self-care is of paramount importance if you want to be able to fulfill all of your responsibilities to the best of your ability. Always remember to take care of yourself first. You won't be able to hold anyone else up if your own legs are shaky.

Newborn Concerns

There's no doubt that the first few weeks and months of parenting can be the hardest. In addition to the anxiety surrounding not knowing what to do, you're also probably sleep-deprived and faced with an infant who's unable to communicate their needs effectively.

Let's look at three common problems new parents deal with when it comes to newborn care and some solutions you might be able to use to solve them.

Feeding Problems

Newborns might struggle to feed for many reasons. A premature baby is likely to experience difficulty feeding because they haven't yet properly developed the ability to suck and swallow milk. This should resolve itself over time, but make sure to regularly follow up with your doctor if you're concerned.

Poor feeding may also be related to illness. Sometimes, if your baby is suffering from an infection like jaundice, ear infection, teething, diarrhea, or a cough, these conditions can make feeding uncomfortable or even painful for your baby. Make sure you see a doctor to rule out any of these conditions as possible causes for their poor feeding. Usually, their feeding difficulties will disappear once the infection has healed.

Another possible reason for poor feeding might be your partner's milk supply. If they're stressed, it can affect the taste of their milk, making the baby less interested in feeding. If your partner is taking any medications that pass through to their breastmilk, this could also affect the baby's desire to feed. You should also ask your partner to avoid using any skin creams or scented lotions on their nipples because that could be putting the baby off as well.

Should your partner fail to get the baby to latch or your baby doesn't appear to be getting an adequate amount of milk per feeding, you might consider trying formula. You don't need to switch to formula exclusively, but supplementing your feedings with formula is a good way to ensure the baby is meeting their nutritional needs.

Sleep Difficulties

When you consider how much time newborns spend sleeping, it's shocking how difficult getting them to sleep can prove to be sometimes! There are a myriad of reasons why you might be struggling to get your baby to sleep, but thankfully, there are some simple solutions you can use to try and solve the problem.

Remember that a baby isn't born with an internal clock that tells them when it's day or night, so you need to teach them. Make sure they're exposed to sunlight during the day so they can begin to develop their circadian rhythm. You can further help by keeping the room where they sleep dark at night and getting blackout curtains if necessary. Avoid exposing them to artificial lights, especially around bedtime.

Introducing a bedtime routine is also a good way to help them begin to understand that it's time for them to start winding down and preparing to sleep. Create an environment for them that is conducive to sleep, and play white noise if necessary. Help ease their tiredness, and make sure you watch for their tired cues. An overtired baby is a cranky baby!

Colic

Just the mention of the word colic is enough to send shivers down the spine of any parent who's had to suffer through it. Colic is when a baby cries uncontrollably for no reason and can last hours on end. This can go on for months. Months!

Colic is defined as when an otherwise healthy baby cries for more than three hours in a day and is impossible to settle or soothe. This pattern needs to be repeated for at least three days a week for at least three weeks. As you can imagine, it's not exactly a fun experience.

The onset of colic is normally around three to four weeks, peaking between six and eight weeks. It lasts until the baby is around four to six months old. If your baby cries uncontrollably for hours on end, make sure to consult with your doctor to make sure it isn't the result of an underlying medical condition such as eczema. Should it turn out that your baby does indeed have colic, the bad news is that there's nothing you can do to stop it.

Colic will understandably cause you a lot of distress, and you may find yourself feeling angry and frustrated. My advice is to get yourself a pair of noise-canceling headphones as you prepare to ride out the storm. Take turns with your partner holding the baby, knowing full well that your efforts will be in vain. Or put your baby in the crib for a while so they can cry it out. I promise they'll be fine.

Balancing Work, Personal Life, and Parenthood

Handling all of your responsibilities might feel like an impossible juggling act at first, but with time and patience, you'll eventually get the hang of it. Wanting to be an involved father is admirable, but sometimes it can feel like you're spreading yourself out too thin when it comes to still being able to get your work done.

Below, I'll offer you a few tips that helped me finally achieve a healthy work-life balance:

- Be present: This means when you're at work, focus on your work and don't try to micromanage what's going on at home. And, when you're at home, focus on your family. Make the most of the time you have with them. Try not to bring work home unless it's absolutely necessary.
- Prioritize things: Sometimes the things you want to get done will have to take a backseat to the things you need to get done. Not everything is of equal importance.
- Give yourself grace: You're not always going to get it right. Sometimes you'll find that one area of your life is thriving while another is lacking a bit, and that's okay.
- Quality over quantity: Even if you can't dedicate as much time to your family as you wish you could, make sure the time you do spend with them counts. Turn off your phone and engage with them. Bond with your baby and be attentive to your partner. They'll appreciate an hour of quality time over the three hours you spend glued to your phone.
- Manage your time effectively: Using things like calendars and schedules will help you make sure that you have enough time to complete everything you need to get done.

Set aside time for your family and stick to the guidelines you've created for yourself.

It's important to remember that you're never going to have it all worked out perfectly. You might need to have a talk with your boss about cutting down your workload or delegating certain tasks to other team members. You might need to tell your partner that you may not be available for certain things. In the end, you just need to find a balance that works for you.

Self-Care for Dads

When it comes to parenting, a lot of us neglect ourselves. Suddenly, your life isn't just about you anymore and you've become so focused on providing for your family that you leave little or no time for yourself. Self-care can feel selfish; however, it's anything but. Remember that you can't pour from an empty flask so in order to be the best father, you first need to be your best self. The only way to do that is to make sure that you're taken care of.

The concept of self-care might conjure up images of yoga retreats and drum circles but it's not a phrase that's only reserved for hippies and chakra huns. Self-care can be as simple as looking after your health. Make sure you're eating nutritious foods and getting enough water. After all, you'll need to be at your healthiest to perform at your optimal capacity.

Getting enough sleep might sound like a myth right now, but at least make sure you're getting enough to be able to think and focus throughout your day. Sure, maybe you won't be getting a full eight hours for the first while, but getting a good few ahead of work wouldn't be a bad idea. Maybe split the night feeds in such a way that you get the first shift and your partner takes the second. You can take over in the early morning while preparing for work so she can get a few extra minutes.

Exercising regularly is also an important aspect of self-care. You'll need to be fit to keep up with a busy toddler! Even if you can't get to the gym for an hour every day anymore, going for a jog around the block a couple of days a week is better than nothing.

Remember to take time out for yourself as well, to do things you enjoy. Catch up with your friends and reach out to other dads for advice. Build yourself a strong support network that you can lean on when you start to get overwhelmed. As much as you and your partner are a team, sometimes getting an outside perspective on things also helps. You might not always see and experience things the same way your partner does. Especially if you've become the only working parent.

Lastly, but most importantly, *do not neglect your mental health.* Parenting is stressful, and life is stressful. There's nothing wrong with admitting it when you need a little support for yourself. Staying mentally sharp is the only way you're going to cope with all these changes and not cave under the weight of all the expectations.

Becoming a father is a massive transition, one that will take a lot out of you. But it's also one that will make you a stronger man than you were before. Don't shy away from the challenges; empower yourself with the knowledge and skills you'll need to overcome them. And remember not to neglect yourself.

CONCLUSION

The experience of fatherhood is impossible to describe in words. It's a journey that will change you fundamentally as a person. You will be tested in more ways than you can imagine, and you'll be pushed to your absolute limits. Despite the challenges you may face, it's probably going to be one of the most incredible and fulfilling experiences of your life.

The journey from pregnancy to childbirth can feel like an eternity. While your baby is growing in your partner's womb, you might feel like an outsider. Find ways to get involved, attend scans, and help plan and decorate the nursery. Show enthusiasm and excitement when all your partner can talk about is the baby for weeks on end. Find ways to bond with your baby while they're in the womb. Talk to them and sing to them. Put your hand on her belly to feel the baby kick. Remember that your partner's hormones are driving the bus, so don't take things too personally. She's probably just as confused by her emotional rollercoaster as you are. Find ways to use this pregnancy as a way to strengthen and deepen your relationship with your partner. Make the most of these last few months you'll have alone before you become parents. Don't shy away from having tough conversations about things like parenting styles or finances. The best way to be a good parent is to work as a team.

When the big day finally arrives, be prepared. Have all your bases covered with regard to the birthing plan and the hospital bag, and make sure you've installed the car seat well in advance. Whether you choose to be right by her side or wait patiently in the waiting room, make sure that the role you play is one you've both agreed to and are comfortable with. Nothing can prepare you for the moment you first lay eyes on your child, and nothing will ever be the same from that moment on.

Dealing with a newborn is both terrifying and gratifying. Try to be as involved in caring for them as possible. Just because your wife is breastfeeding doesn't mean you can't still actively participate in the responsibility of caring for the baby. Help with changing diapers, burping, and soothing the baby. Make the most of any opportunity you get to bond with the baby. You'll be surprised at how fast those early days fly by, although it may not feel that way at first.

Watching your baby grow and develop is such an amazing experience. Witnessing each of their milestones and celebrating their achievements will make you feel emotions you didn't even know were possible. Seeing them start to develop their own personalities, tastes, and preferences is truly a remarkable journey. It's like you blink, and suddenly, this helpless newborn has become a toddler. Cherish all of these moments because you'll never get them again. Becoming a father is about so much more than just taking on a new responsibility. It's about realizing the important things in life and making the most of every moment.

Appreciate your partner because pregnancy and childbirth will give you a whole new level of respect and admiration for them. Be as supportive as you can, understanding how taxing this journey can be and how much it's taking out of them. Be the father you wish you had, even if you're not sure what that looks like right now. Reach out to people for support and advice; it's okay not to have all the answers. Don't be afraid to talk about your feelings, whether that's with your partner or a therapist. And don't be too hard on yourself. Despite the fact that you will never be an ideal father, I am certain you will be an excellent one.

REFERENCES

Advantages and Disadvantages of Home Birth. (n.d.). AspiringYouths. Retrieved February 19, 2024, from https://aspiringyouths.com/advantages-disadvantages/home-birth/

Advice for Dad Feeding Baby: 7 Bottle Feeding Tips for Dad. (2023, June 15). Https://Milk-Drunk.com/. https://milk-drunk.com/advice-for-new-dads-formula-feeding/

American Academy of Pediatrics. (2023, August 21). *Safe sleep.* AAP. https://www.aap.org/en/patient-care/safe-sleep/

Anita. (2018, May 9). *How to tell when baby wants to play.* Mum's Grapevine. https://mumsgrapevine.com.au/2018/05/when-baby-wants-to-play/

Baby basics: How to burp your baby. (n.d.). UNICEF. https://www.unicef.org/parenting/child-care/how-to-burp-baby

Baby cues and baby body language: a guide. (n.d.). Raising Children Network. https://raisingchildren.net.au/newborns/connecting-communicating/communicating/baby-cues

Baby Development Stages in the First Year: Month by Month. (2019, September 18). Healthline. https://www.healthline.com/health/baby/baby-development-stages

Baby's Hunger Cues | WIC Breastfeeding. (n.d.). Wicbreastfeeding.. https://wicbreastfeeding.fns.usda.gov/babys-hunger-cues

What To Pack In Your Hospital Bag When You Have A Baby. (2021, January 11). BabyYumYum. https://www.babyyumyum.co.za/what-to-pack-in-your-hospital-bag-when-you-have-a-baby/

Bailik, M. (2018, August 1). *40 Best Parenting Quotes of All Time.* Momtastic. https://www.momtastic.com/parenting/541137-40-amazing-quotes-parenthood/

Barker, J. (n.d.). *Dad's To-Do List: Getting Ready for Baby.* WebMD. https://www.webmd.com/baby/dads-to-do-list-getting-ready-for-baby

Barnes, C. (2022, September 29). *Five Ways Your Partner Can Support You During Postpartum.* Hello Postpartum. https://hellopostpartum.com/partner-support-postpartum/

Bartha, C. (2022, July 24). *Dads and Childbirth: 31 Tips For Dads During Labor and Delivery.* Wellandgood Family. https://wellandgoodfamily.com/31-tips-for-dads-during-labor-and-childbirth/

Benefits of skin-to-skin contact with your newborn. (2021). BabyCenter.

https://www.babycenter.com/baby/newborn-baby/benefits-of-skin-to-skin-contact-with-your-newborn_20005036

Bonding is essential for normal infant development. (n.d.). News. https://health.uc-davis.edu/news/headlines/bonding-is-essential-for-normal-infant-development/2010/01

Buckley, M. (n.d.). *45 Inspirational Dad Quotes About Parenting.* Regain. https://www.regain.us/advice/parenting/45-inspirational-dad-quotes-about-parenting/

Budgeting for New Parents: How to Budget for Baby. (n.d.). NerdWallet. https://www.nerdwallet.com/article/finance/baby-budget-new-parents

Carlos, J. P. (2023, July 15). *How to Change Baby Diapers: A Step-by-Step Survival Guide for Dads.* WeHaveKids. https://wehavekids.com/parenting/Changing-Diapers-A-Step-by-Step-Survival-Guide-for-Dads

Changing Diapers. (n.d.). Dads Adventure. https://dadsadventure.com/changing-diapers/

Cheever, S. (2020, July 8). *100 Pregnancy Quotes (Beautiful & Inspirational).* Mom Loves Best; Mom Loves Best. https://momlovesbest.com/pregnancy-quotes

Church, E. (2023, January 2). *100 Newborn Quotes to Make You Smile.* Baby Chick. https://www.baby-chick.com/newborn-baby-quotes-to-make-you-smile/

Co-Sleeping With Your Baby. (2022, October 4). Sleep Foundation. https://www.sleepfoundation.org/baby-sleep/co-sleeping#tips-and-precautions-for-safer-co-sleeping-4

Coxon, L. (2017, October 25). *6 ways to support a mother who has postpartum depression.* Today's Parent. https://www.todaysparent.com/family/womens-health/ways-to-support-a-mother-who-has-postpartum-depression/

Dad' Dad's Guide to s Guide to. (n.d.). Texasattorneygeneral. Retrieved February 19, 2024, from https://www.texasattorneygeneral.gov/sites/default/files/files/child-support/Publications/13-06-15131DadsGuidetoFatherhood-ACC.pdf

De Bellefonds, C. (2022). *Baby milestones month by month.* BabyCenter. https://www.babycenter.com/baby/baby-development/baby-milestones-1-to-6-months_1496585

6 easy self-care tips for dads. (2023, June 26). Didofy. https://didofy.com/parenting-advice/6-easy-self-care-tips-for-dads

Elsayed, S. (2022, December 3). *100 baby first steps quotes & walk quotes to celebrate their milestones.* Babylic. https://www.babylic.com/baby-first-steps-quotes/

8 (Realistic) Ways Working Dads Can Achieve Work-Life Balance. (n.d.). Ivyexec. https://ivyexec.com/career-advice/2022/8-realistic-ways-working-dads-can-achieve-work-life-balance

Engqvist, I., & Nilsson, K. (2011). Men's experience of their partners' postpartum psychiatric disorders: narratives from the internet. *Mental Health in Family Medicine, 8*(3), 137–146. https://www.ncbi.nlm.nih.gov/pmc/articles/PMC3314270

Expectant Fathers: Becoming a Dad | Pampers. (n.d.). Web-Pampers-US-EN. https://www.pampers.com/en-us/pregnancy/pregnancy-symptoms/article/expectant-fathers-symptoms-and-challenges

Finding Fatherhood: The Transition to Being A Dad. (2018, April 27). Zencare Blog. https://blog.zencare.co/adjusting-to-fatherhood/

First-time dad tips—how to be a hands-on dad. (n.d.). Smababy. https://www.smababy.co.uk/pregnancy/tips-on-being-a-first-time-dad

Fries, W. C. (2010, January 20). *10 Steps to Help Prevent SIDS.* WebMD. https://www.webmd.com/parenting/sids-prevention

Gregory, N. (2024, February 15). *5 Best Morning Sickness Remedies, According To Experts.* Forbes Health. https://www.forbes.com/health/womens-health/pregnancy/best-morning-sickness-remedies/

Hanson, S., Hunter, L. P., Bormann, J. R., & Sobo, E. J. (2009). Paternal Fears of Childbirth: A Literature Review. *Journal of Perinatal Education, 18*(4), 12–20. https://doi.org/10.1624/105812409x474672

Health Features Archives. (n.d.). CHOC Children's. Retrieved February 19, 2024, from https://kidshealth.org/CHOC/en/parents/burping.html

Healthy relationships with partners in pregnancy. (n.d.). Raising Children Network. https://raisingchildren.net.au/pregnancy/pregnancy-for-partners/relationships-and-feelings/healthy-relationships-with-partners-pregnancy

Hospital bag checklist for labour | Huggies® South Africa. (n.d.). Huggies. Retrieved February 19, 2024, from https://www.huggies.co.za/new-born/childbirth/preparing-for-childbirth

How (and Why) to Create a Birth Plan. (n.d.). What to Expect. https://www.whattoexpect.com/pregnancy/labor-and-delivery/birth-plan/

How Dads Can Support Their Breastfeeding Partner. (n.d.). Wicbreastfeeding. https://wicbreastfeeding.fns.usda.gov/how-dads-can-support-their-breastfeeding-partner

How Do You Tell If a Baby Is Hungry or Wants Comfort? (2022, October 3). Sangpediatrics. https://www.sangpediatrics.com/how-do-you-tell-if-a-baby-is-hungry-or-wants-comfort

How Partners Can Support Postpartum. (n.d.). Hey, Sleepy Baby. Retrieved February 19, 2024, from https://heysleepybaby.com/blog/how-partners-can-support-birthing-parents-postpartum

How To Clean & Sanitize Baby Bottles (Simple Guide). (n.d.). Baby Schooling. Retrieved February 18, 2024, from https://www.babyschooling.com/learning-center/feeding-guides/clean-sanitize-baby-bottles/

How to Clean, Sanitize, and Store Infant Feeding Items. (2022, June 15). Centers for

Disease Control and Prevention. https://www.cdc.gov/hygiene/child-care/clean-sanitize.html

How to help a partner with postpartum depression or anxiety. (2019, August 15). HealthPartners Blog. https://www.healthpartners.com/blog/postpartum-depression-or-anxiety/

How to Increase Breast Milk: Home Remedies, Diet, Supplements. (2018, May 7). Healthline. https://www.healthline.com/health/parenting/how-to-increase-breast-milk

How to Make a Baby Bottle: Storage and More. (n.d.). Similac. Retrieved February 19, 2024, from https://www.similac.com/baby-feeding/formula-guide/how-to-make-a-bottle.html

How to Make a Baby Bottle: What You Need to Know. (n.d.). Nutritionnews. Retrieved February 18, 2024, from https://www.nutritionnews.abbott/pregnancy-childhood/infant-toddler/how-to-make-a-baby-bottle--what-you-need-to-know/

How to Prepare Your Relationship for Baby. (2019, August 6). Thebump. https://www.thebump.com/a/prepare-your-relationship-for-baby

Johnson, T, C. (n.d.). *How to Create a Birth Plan.* WebMD. https://www.webmd.com/baby/how-to-create-a-birth-plan

Incorporating Self Care Into Your Routine as a Parent. (2023, July 26). Dear Fathers. https://dearfathers.com/2023/07/incorporating-self-care-into-your-routine-as-a-parent/

Infant sleep problems: A troubleshooting guide. (2017, January 2). PARENTING SCIENCE. https://parentingscience.com/infant-sleep-problems/

Is This Postpartum Depression? And If So, What Can I Do? (2016, August 29). Psych Central. https://psychcentral.com/depression/postpartum-depression

Ismail, A. (2021, December 13). *The Dangerous Pattern One Therapist Sees in New Fathers.* Slate. https://slate.com/human-interest/2021/12/new-dad-depression-trend-therapy-help.html

January 10, A. B., & 2020. (2020, January 10). *How to support your wife or partner after birth.* Today's Parent. https://www.todaysparent.com/baby/postpartum-care/how-to-support-your-wife-after-birth/

Keeping Your Baby Safe While Sleeping. (n.d.). Tennessee Health. https://www.tn.gov/content/dam/tn/health/documents/SafeSleep_FlipChart.pdf

Krieger, L. (2022, May 16). *9 Things to Do to Get Your House in Order Before Baby Comes.* Parents. https://www.parents.com/pregnancy/my-life/preparing-for-baby/9-things-to-do-to-get-your-house-in-order-before-baby-comes/

Learning your baby's cues. (n.d.). Marchofdimes. https://www.marchofdimes.org/find-support/topics/neonatal-intensive-care-unit-nicu/learning-your-babys-cues

Making a great start to parenthood: tips for non-birthing parents. (n.d.). Raising Children

Network. https://raisingchildren.net.au/pregnancy/pregnancy-for-part-ners/early-parenting/great-start-to-parenthood-non-birthing-parents-tips

Postpartum depression. (2019, March). March of Dimes. https://www.mar-chofdimes.org/find-support/topics/postpartum/postpartum-depression

Stages of Labor and birth: Baby, it's time! (2022, January 13). Mayo Clinic. https://www.mayoclinic.org/healthy-lifestyle/labor-and-delivery/in-depth/stages-of-labor/art-20046545

Mitchell, M. (n.d.). *Childbirth Quotes (161 quotes).* Goodreads. Retrieved February 19, 2024, from https://www.goodreads.com/quotes/tag/childbirth

Morin, A. (2022). *Developmental Milestones From Birth to Age 1.* Understood. https://www.understood.org/en/articles/developmental-milestones-from-birth-to-age-1

Nabar, D. A., & Bellani, P, S. (n.d.). *Normal delivery procedure step-by-step: photos.* BabyCenter India. https://www.babycenter.in/l1026533/normal-delivery-procedure-step-by-step-photos

Nguyen, H. (2021, September 29). *Postpartum recovery: What to expect.* HealthPart-ners Blog. https://www.healthpartners.com/blog/what-to-expect-after-giving-birth/

Nurturing Your Relationship During Pregnancy. (n.d.). What to Expect. https://www.whattoexpect.com/pregnancy/ask-heidi/week-10/nurturing-your-relationship.aspx

Osterland, A. (2022, March 28). *Budgeting for a baby: Here's what financial advisors recommend for new parents.* CNBC. https://www.cnbc.com/2022/03/28/budget-ing-for-baby-what-financial-advisors-recommend-for-new-parents.html

Partner Support During Pregnancy. (n.d.). Myhealth.alberta.ca. https://myhealth.al-berta.ca/Health/Pages/conditions.aspx?hwid=abp7352&lang=en-ca

Pfeiffer, J. (2023, September 18). *Heartfelt Pregnancy Quotes For Daddy: Celebrating Fatherhood.* The Fifth Element Life. https://thefifthelementlife.com/pregnancy-quotes-for-daddy/

Pittman, F. (n.d.). *TOP 25 BECOMING A FATHER QUOTES.* A-Z Quotes. Retrieved February 19, 2024, from https://www.azquotes.com/quotes/topics/becoming-a-father.html

Poor Feeding in Infants: Causes, Emergency Care & Treatments. (2016, February 16). Healthline. https://www.healthline.com/health/poor-feeding-in-infants

Postnatal depression Causes, Symptoms & Treatment. (n.d.). Clicks. https://clicks.-co.za/health/conditions/article-view/postnatal-depression

Pregnancy Week by Week. (n.d.). Marchofdimes. https://www.mar-chofdimes.org/pregnancy-week-week#33

Preparing for a baby together. (n.d.). Mayo Clinic Health System. https://www.mayoclinichealthsystem.org/hometown-health/speaking-of-health/preparing-for-a-baby-together

Preparing for Fatherhood: 25 Tips for Dads-to-Be. (n.d.). Pampers. https://www.pampers.com/en-us/pregnancy/preparing-for-your-new-baby/article/preparing-for-fatherhood

Prior, E. (2020, October 12). *10 ways to be an (emotionally) supportive husband during pregnancy.* Professional-Counselling. https://www.professional-counselling.com/how-to-be-a-supportive-husband-during-pregnancy.html

Rae, M., Cox, C., & Dingel, H. (2022, July 13). *Health costs associated with pregnancy, childbirth, and postpartum care.* Peterson-KFF Health System Tracker. https://www.healthsystemtracker.org/brief/health-costs-associated-with-pregnancy-childbirth-and-postpartum-care/

Rockliffe, L. (2023, March 10). *The importance of social support in pregnancy and ways to connect with others.* Tommy's. https://www.tommys.org/pregnancy-information/pregnancy-news-blogs/pregnancy-news-blogs-being-pregnant/importance-social-support

Rogers, L. (2022, June 13). *Week by week pregnancy advice for expecting dads and partners.* What to Expect. https://www.whattoexpect.com/pregnancy/for-dad/week-by-week-pregnancy-advice-dads-partners/

Sarah. (n.d.). *Sarah's story.* PANDA. https://panda.org.au/stories/sarahs-story/

Setting up a Nursery Guide for Parents With Top Examples. (2019, January 14). Dadprogress.com. https://dadprogress.com/setting-up-nursery/

Sleepy Cues-How Can you Tell When Your Baby is Tired? (n.d.). Hey, Sleepy Baby. Retrieved February 19, 2024, from https://heysleepybaby.com/blog/sleepy-cues-how-can-you-tell-when-your-baby-is-tired

Soleyn, D. (2023, January 27). *Time Management for Dads: Prioritizing what matters and finding balance - Dad Central.* https://dadcentral.ca/time-management-for-dads-prioritizing-what-matters-and-finding-balance/

Stages of Labor. (n.d.). Bidmc. https://www.bidmc.org/centers-and-departments/obstetrics-and-gynecology/programs-and-services/pregnancy/labor-and-delivery/stages-of-labor

Steen, M. (n.d.). *Why is newborn baby skin-to-skin contact with dads and non-birthing parents important? Here's what the science says.* The Conversation. Retrieved March 10, 2023, from https://theconversation.com/why-is-newborn-baby-skin-to-skin-contact-with-dads-and-non-birthing-parents-important-heres-what-the-science-says-188927

Steinem, G. (n.d.). *14 Quotes About Giving Birth That'll Empower You.* Romper. https://www.romper.com/p/14-quotes-about-giving-birth-thatll-empower-you-12797595

Taylor, B. (2017, June 7). *How to cope with a colicky baby*. Direct Advice for Dads. https://directadvicefordads.com.au/new-dads/what-the-hell-is-colic/

Taylor, M. (2021, April 6). *The Pros and Cons of Hospital Birth*. What to Expect. https://www.whattoexpect.com/pregnancy/hospital-birth/

Team, E. (2023, October 4). *How to Still Be Intimate When Pregnant*. Being the Parent. https://www.beingtheparent.com/how-to-still-be-intimate-when-pregnant/

10 Tips for Nurturing Your Relationship During Pregnancy. (2023, December 19). Proven.love. https://proven.love/nurturing-your-relationship-during-pregnancy/

The ABCs of Safe Sleep. (n.d.). Hopkinsmedicine. https://www.hopkinsmedicine.org/news/articles/2022/10/the-abcs-of-safe-sleep

The ABC's of Safe Sleep. (n.d.). Nationwidechildrens. https://www.nationwidechildrens.org/family-resources-education/700childrens/2014/09/the-abcs-of-safe-sleep

The Bump Editors. (2014, August 19). *Baby Proofing Checklist: Before Baby Comes Home*. The Bump. https://www.thebump.com/a/checklist-babyproofing-part-1

The New Dad Guide to Preparing for the Postpartum Phase. (n.d.). Needed. Retrieved February 19, 2024, from https://thisisneeded.com/blogs/postpartum-and-breastfeeding/the-new-dad-guide-to-preparing-for-the-postpartum-phase

The Role of Dads in Postpartum: Partner support is key to managing anxiety. (2015, May 1). Health Journal. https://www.thehealthjournals.com/the-role-of-dads-in-postpartum/amp/

The ultimate rookie dad guide to newborns. (2019, January 9). Today's Parent. https://www.todaysparent.com/baby/newborn-care/a-rookie-dads-guide-to-newborns

Tips for Setting Up Your Baby's Nursery. (n.d.). Verywell Family. https://www.verywellfamily.com/setting-up-the-nursery-284580

Wisner, W. (2021, June 14). *How to support your partner during pregnancy*. Verywell Family. https://www.verywellfamily.com/partner-support-during-pregnancy-4797874

Work-Life Balance For Dads. Tips to Achieve It All. (n.d.). Daduniversity. https://www.daduniversity.com/blog/work-life-balance-for-dads-tips-to-achieve-it-all

Wright, K. (2021, May 3). *The Pros and Cons of Birthing Centers, And Why I Ultimately Chose a Hospital Birth*. Growing Serendipity. https://theexperiencedmama.com/pros-and-cons-of-birthing-centers/

Your decision, my decision, our decision. (2018, September 28). Tonyrobbins. https://www.tonyrobbins.com/love-relationships/your-decision-my-decision-our-decision/